Beyond Covid
The Global
Elite's Plan
for Human 2.0

FIRST PRINTING

Billy Crone

Copyright © 2022
All Rights Reserved

Cover Design:
CHRIS TAYLOR

*To my family, Church family,
and all those around the world
who have had loved ones
murdered from this viral agenda.*

*God will have the last word
on this evil and suffering
and satanic behavior.*

*If these people
do not ask for forgiveness
and get saved
through Jesus Christ,*

*Hell will be there
awaiting them
with open arms.*

Contents

Preface

I think it was at a garage sale where I first came across one of those Chinese boxes. You know, those boxes that you open up and inside is another box, and then inside that box is another box, and so on and so forth? Well, believe it or not, that's an appropriate way to describe the behavior of the Global Elites with their release of the Covid plandemic upon humanity. Just when you thought you understood all, you know, the first box, the more you investigate and open things up, the more boxes or agendas you discover. In fact, the deeper you go, the more you become shocked and appalled at how many well thought out sick, evil and twisted their plans really are. You thought Covid was just about manipulating an election? Open up another box and you'll discover it was also about removing our freedoms. But keep going and you'll open yet another box revealing how it was also a satanic murderous plot to annihilate a large population of the planet. Keep going and you'll spy yet another box revealing how it was also designed to destroy the immune system of those who survive. Persist and you'll come across even more news that it was a sneaky deliberate trick to get people to inject themselves with a man-made technology that can now track, identify, and genetically modify them anywhere on the whole planet. And then, if you have the stomach to continue on from there, you'll even discover other sick boxes inside the original Covid box that these Global Elites actually have plans to create Super Soldiers, Zombies, and a new non-human species, and even worker bees for the so-called Utopia they're building for us, whether we want it or not. And frankly, to be honest with you, I wish none of this were true, but as a truth-teller, a Christian, we have to deal with the facts and warn people of these ungodly dastardly "boxed" plans for humanity and encourage them to take the way out through Jesus Christ. One last piece of advice; when you are through reading this book, will you please READ YOUR BIBLE? I mean that in the nicest possible way. Enjoy, and I'm looking forward to seeing you someday!

Billy Crone
Las Vegas, Nevada
2022

Chapter One

The Exposers of Human 2.0

With a title like ***Beyond Covid: The Global Elite's Plan for Human 2.0***, let's clarify a little bit before you think I went off the deep end. The first part there in the title, ***Beyond Covid***, is to address a concern I have concerning the Covid Plandemic that has not gone away. That's the problem. A lot of people think it has gone away, with all this relaxing of the mask mandates and the lessening of the public restrictions, the allowing of people to go back to buying and selling in stores, the going out to restaurants and other venues, as well as even lessening the mandates for the Covid 19 shots themselves.

Based on this, it would appear to many people that, "As crazy as the last two years were, aren't you glad it's all over?" Or is it? You see, I believe, based upon research and the openly admitted behavior of the Global Elites, they haven't stopped implementing their nefarious global evil plans for us with their manufactured Covid Plandemic that was launched back in 2020. Not at all. Rather, their evil, dastardly plans are still in high gear, even worse than what we've seen so far, and, once again, they're using the power of Mass Media to distract us from looking at this next evil phase of their plan as seen in a video like this:

The video opens with people on an airplane. A woman in a seat is upset and hysterically crying. The stewardess grabs the lady and shakes her saying, "Madam, get hold of yourself!"

In large print over each individual are the words as follows: Over the upset lady is "Our Collective Focus," over the stewardess, "Covid;" and over a gentleman who steps up to help, "Ukraine." The stewardess steps away, and the gentleman that has come to help her, slaps the passenger to get her to come to her senses and calm down, but just as he slaps her, another passenger comes up and pulls the gentleman off the woman. Large letters over the second male passenger read "Will Smith." He tells the gentleman to go sit down, and he will take care of this out-of-control woman.

He proceeds to grab hold of her and shakes her as hard as he can saying, "Get hold of yourself!" Then the next person to come to her aid is a nun. Over her, the words are "Men Can Be Women." But she doesn't seem to be doing any better, because all she is doing is shaking and slapping the poor out-of-control woman. Then all the passengers are lined up to try to calm the woman down. The words over each of them are "White Supremacy," "Cyber Attacks," "Gun Violence," and "January 6th."

And it just keeps going on and on, doesn't it? One distractive topic after another! And if you want to get even more information on how we are being constantly distracted and manipulated by the Media, then get our other documentary entitled, ***Subliminal Seduction: How the Mass Media Mesmerizes the Minds of the Masses***.

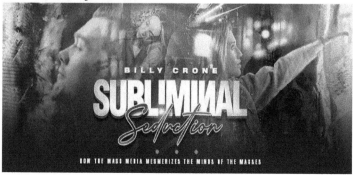

But as you can see, the media is just one big, mass global distraction tool that enables the Global Elites to move forward unhindered with their dastardly plans to enslave us, humanity. They do it all behind the scenes, while we keep looking over here or there, anywhere but at what they're really doing, totally distracted from the next, never-ending news cycle that's designed to keep us blinded to the facts and what's really going on behind the scenes.

This is what I want to address. The Global Elite's plans *Beyond Covid*. They haven't stopped. So, what are they planning next? Now, if you haven't already seen it, I encourage you to get another one of our resources *The Great Covid Deception* where we dealt with the Global Elite's plans, that they have already implemented upon us, with the Covid Plandemic.

Again, the Global Elite's plans are still marching forward. Even beyond what we covered in that documentary, and we're simply being distracted, and dare I say, lulled to sleep over it with all the seemingly lessening of their Covid restrictions.

But secondly, I also wanted to address the other half of that title, *The Global Elite's Plan for Human 2.0*. Just when you thought it couldn't get any worse. This is just some of the plans they are getting ready to implement upon us, even way *Beyond* what they've already accomplished with Covid over the last two years of restrictions and violations of our God given freedoms.

Believe it or not, these same Elites want to annihilate, alter, and enhance humanity into what and how they think we should be, according to their image, not God's. And as wild as that sounds, this is what I wanted to cover in the following interview.

What you are about to see, is a discussion between several legal and medical professionals and experts, who have come together collectively over this Covid Plandemic agenda. They started a legal think tank called The Corona Investigative Committee. And they're not lightweights either, nor are they a bunch of tinfoil, triangle hat wearing people. Rather, they are a serious group of legal and medical experts who state why they exist.[1]

And I quote, *"Since mid-July 2020, The Corona Investigative Committee has been conducting live, multi-hour sessions to investigate why federal and state governments (around the world) have imposed unprecedented restrictions, as part of the Coronavirus response, and what the consequences have been and still are for people."*

In other words, the agenda has never stopped! Yes, they've got us focused on gun control, Ukraine, Russia, Russia, Russia, Will Smith, gender issues, or a plethora of other distractions, but this doesn't mean these Elites have finished the job of what they ultimately want to do to humanity with this pre-planned Covid Plandemic.

The Corona Investigative Committee *"has now begun legal proceedings against the CDC, the WHO, and the Bill and Melinda Gates Foundation, as well as the Davos Group, for crimes against humanity, genocide, violations of the Nuremberg Code and for misleading the world about the coronavirus pandemic."*

So, I say that to show you that these people are serious. And what we're going to do is dissect the following interview from them in one of their weekly updates, and put it to the test, to see if what they're saying is true, as wild and disturbing and evil as it sounds.

In fact, that's exactly what the Bible says we should do, especially with matters of grave importance. It's called being a Berean. We don't take anything at face value. We always put it to the test like the Bereans did.

Acts 17:10-12 "As soon as it was night, the brothers sent Paul and Silas away to Berea. On arriving there, they went to the Jewish synagogue. Now the Bereans were of more noble character than the Thessalonians, for they received the message with great eagerness and examined the Scriptures every day to see if what Paul said was true. Many of the Jews believed, as did also a number of prominent Greek women and many Greek men."

Before the Bereans were going to believe anything, even what the Apostle Paul said about Jesus, they were diligent to test it out by searching the rest of the Scriptures. In other words, they did their homework in order to verify if Paul's claims about eternal matters were true.

So, that's what we're going to do in this book. We're not going to take anybody's words at face value. We're going to test them. We're going to search it out and see, if in fact, this is really what's going on, as sick and evil as it is. And that sick and evil plan is this. "Are the Global Elites really planning on going even Beyond Covid, and what they've already accomplished, to now create a world full of Zombies, Super Soldiers, and a bunch of Human Cattle?" I know it sounds insane, but let's be those Bereans and begin to investigate the facts. And let's do that by first introducing the cast.

The first person is this man, Dr. Reiner Fuellmich. He is featured in the background of this video shot. He's been an Attorney at Law since 1993 in Germany, as well as in California since 1994. And since 1991 he's also been a Consumer Protection Attorney, especially against the banks. Then from 1985–2001 he was the Scientific Assistant to Professor Deutsch at the University of Göttingen, Research Center for Medical and Pharmaceutical Law, and a member of the Ethics Committees of the University Hospitals of Göttingen and Hannover.

The next person is this lady, Viviane Fischer, who is leading the interview process. And she too is an Attorney at Law and an Economist, as well as a Business lawyer in Berlin, and she is active in the

protection of fundamental human rights.

Then we have the main character, if you will, being interviewed by The Corona Investigative Committee, and that's this guy, Todd Callender.

He is a Lawyer and Disabled Rights Advocate who has worked in the disability, health, and life insurance industry for more than 20 years. He focuses on the international convergence of biomedical, morbidity and mortality risks in the global legal context.

He was the first lawyer in the United States to sue the US Department of Defense, the HHS, and the FDA in relation to the Covid mandates, and as such, he acquired 400,000 military clients (or plaintiffs) with scores of them, and others, that have provided ample whistleblower evidence of what's really going on in the military over the jab. Todd also knows, from the DMED Database (the Defense Medical Epidemiology Database), that in 10 months of 2021, all cause morbidity and mortality has increased by 11,000%, between the ages of 18-40 years for military personnel. And as Todd puts it: "This is Genocide."

Chapter Two

The Genocide of Human 2.0

So, now that we've established the cast, let's begin our investigative Berean journey, checking out the facts, dissecting this conversation about what the Global Elites are planning on doing, even way Beyond the current Covid agenda that we've dealt with so far. Let's begin, shall we?

Viviane Fischer: *"Now we turn to another guest. We have a lawyer, Todd Callender. There is something very interesting that you discovered like when you worked with the Department of Defense and the Covid vaccine injection aftermath."*

Todd Callender: *"It really all started twenty plus years ago when I was working in the vaccine industry. My family owned the original property rights to the needle-free mass vaccination device. So, I spent three years in the third phase of the clinical field trials, the same ones they are having with these purported vaccines right now. I learned a lot about the vaccine industry insomuch that I have been in business now with these very same people that are now executing this genocide. So, I do understand that and why it is that I filed suit against the DOD, the Health and Human Services, and the FDA in August of last year.*

When I saw what was happening, including the Pandemic bond that the World Bank and IMF put together, they use the claim on that 500 million denominated in SDR (Special Drawing Rights). It was the first time that they had made the SDR into a cryptocurrency. When that happened, it made sense to me that they were simply implementing the 2005 International Health Regulations in order to provide a global homogenized response as to what it was that they had created. And when you support what was authorized by the Secretary, I realized it was a global military operation, and it would be forced onto humanity.

So, I just couldn't help it, I just had to file suit. The point of filing suit, as much as anything, is to educate the U.S. military that what it is that they are purporting to do is illegal per the Nuremberg Code and International Convention on Civil and Political Rights, per the International Convention of Human Rights and per the Uniform Military Code of Military Justice and U.S. statutes. All of this is patently illegal. We all know that, and I was shocked by how it is that nobody in government, or pretty much in any governments of the world stage, seems to care, minus a few exceptions. This is a very well-coordinated genocide in progress."

Whoa! Wait a second. Let's stop right there. Is the Covid Plandemic, and the shots being administered, really by a "well-coordinated effort to create mass genocide" across the whole planet by Global entities?

Yes, let's put it to the test. Let's be a Berean. This is what we exposed in our other documentary mentioned earlier, ***The Great Covid Deception.*** Other people, besides Todd, exposed the Global Mass Genocide motive, including many secular doctors as well. In fact, here's just two examples of the Mass Genocide that they say is really coming very soon as a result of the Covid shots.

The first one is a warning by Dr. Vladimir Zelenko. He is one of the world's leading medical experts on the Covid shots and protocols, and he simply calls them for what they are, they are "Poison Death Shots." Let's listen in.

Dr. Zelenko: *"I just want to summarize it, that there is no need for this vaccine. There is no need for protection for anyone and I'll explain. Children are already protected with a 99.998% chance of getting better. Young adults from 18 to 45 have a 99.95% chance of getting better. This is according to the CDC. Someone who already had Covid and has the antibodies, naturally-induced immunity is a billion times more effective than artificially induced immunity through the vaccine.*

So, why would I vaccinate someone with a poison death shot that is inferior, with dangerous antibodies, when I already have heathy antibodies? And then when you look at the high risks of the population that has a 7.5% death rate, to my data, the first in the world, which I published, that has become the basis of over 200 other studies, and I have corroborated my observations that if you treat people in the right timeframe, you reduce that rate by 85%. So, out of 600,000 Americans, we could have prevented 510,000 from going to the hospital and dying. Oh, and by the way, I presented this information to BiBi Netanyahu directly into his hands in April 2020. I informed every single member of your Ministry of Health as well. So, my question to you is, if I can reduce the death rate by 7.5% or less than half of a percent, why would I use a poison death shot that doesn't work and has tremendous and horrendous side effects?

Now I will go over my experiments with you. If everyone on the planet were to get Covid and not get treated, the death rate globally will be less than half of a percent. Now I'm not advocating for that. There are a lot of people, 35 million people that would die. However, if you follow the advice of some of the global leaders, like Bill Gates said last year, 7 billion people need to be vaccinated, the death rate will be over 2 billion people. So, wake up! This is World War Three. This is the level of malfeasance and malevolence that we have not seen probably since the history of humanity."

Okay, well, 2 billion people haven't died yet, so he must have got it wrong, right? Wrong! There are three phases of deaths from these Covid shots that Dr. Zelenko shares. The first phase is called the Acute Death Phase, where people will die within a few hours or days from the poison death shots. Then there's the second phase called Sub Acute Death, where people will die within just a few weeks or months, which by the way has become the new norm for even healthy people and athletes who got the shots, as seen here.

Headlines: *"Inside the $250 million effort to convince Americans the coronavirus vaccines are safe." "Social Media Influencer Admits Being Offered Money to Promote Vaccines." "White House has enlisted dozens of TikTokers, YouTubers, and Twitch streamers to encourage young Americans to get vaccinated." "America's Health Will Soon Be in the Hands of Very Minor Internet Celebrities."*

CBS News Reports: *"Billed as one of the largest education campaigns ever. President Biden's chief medical advisor said, 'People need trusted messengers.' The White House has now recruited TikTokers, YouTubers and more. The goal is, 'Get Americans to get the Covid vaccine.'"*

Commercial number one: Opens with a man jumping out of bed, full of excitement. "I'm getting the vaccine today!" He runs into his daughter's room and exclaims, "It's vaccination day!" He then runs to the window, opens it up and yells to the neighborhood, "It's vaccination day!"

Commercial number two: Shows a cartoon where a young man is also very happy. He is walking out of the doctor's office singing, "Today I got my Covid jab, and I'm feeling really fab. I am so happy. I have been waiting for this day."

Commercial number three: The words CORONAVIRUS-19 is printed across the screen. Rapper Juvenile spells out the letters and then tells the audience that they have to get the shot from Pfizer by BioNTech. ("Pfizer and Moderna Covid vaccines 95% effective in clinical trials" prints on the screen as he is singing.) The name of the song is "Vax that Thang Up" to encourage Covid-19 vaccinations to the younger generation.

Commercial number four: Three guys dressed in tuxes are harmonizing and holding a large syringe. "Get your shot with your syringe. Stick it in me like you really mean it." They are singing it to the tune of "Mr. Sandman."

Commercial number five: This commercial looks like Michael Jackson dancing in the front room, but it sounds like the BeeGees in the background singing "Get your shot, get your shot," to the tune of "Staying alive, staying alive."

Commercial number six: This commercial has a clip from *The Lion King*, and they are singing, "I just can't wait to get my vaccine," with the tune of the theme song from the movie.

Commercial number seven: Here we have some people dancing in the parking lot. They are singing, "Now's the time to vaccinate, look at your watch, there's no time to wait!"

Commercial number eight: A girl is sitting in the chair with her sleeve rolled up, ready for the shot. This is filmed in India, so it's not in English, but the message comes across that the shot is what you should have. An Indian doctor comes up to her with a needle, and he gives her the shot.

Commercial number 9: Anderson Cooper is dancing down the street and singing, "The vaccine's on its way!"

Multiple Newscaster Reports: "A high school senior collapses on the tennis court."

"Breaking News: Details on the death of a high school soccer player."

"Finland, Denmark star man, Chris Erickson, collapsed after the first half."

"The community is mourning tonight after a high school player died."

"One high school football player died after collapsing on the field during football practice."

"Star college basketball player collapses on the court. We have to warn you, the video may be difficult to watch."

"A West Catholic high school student has died after collapsing during a football scrimmage."

"At mile eight, she suddenly felt fuzzy and blacked out."

"Seventeen-year-old Ryan Jacob's heart stopped."

"Megan went into cardiac arrest."

Newspaper Headlines:

"Florida high school football player dies after collapsing during practice."

"Josh Downie: Cricketer, 24, dies after heart attack at practice."

"An 18-year-old Hungarian football player collapsed on the field and died."

"He collapsed in the middle of a game."

"Footballer collapsed in match."

"PA. boy, 12, collapses, dies at middle school basketball practice."

"Jens, 27 collapses on the football field and dies."

"Latin-American tour suffers another tragic loss after caddie collapses and dies."

"C-League: Player collapses, game in Flammersbach ends."

"After a collapse on the pitch: 17-year-old soccer player on the mend."

"Danish second division player, Wessam Abou Ali, collapses on the pitch – the game is abandoned."

"The reason for his collapse is unknown."

"The reason why Manny collapsed in the first place, still isn't known."

"Kjeld Nuis very sick after vaccination: 'The body is not cooperating.'"

"24-year-old hockey player dies after collapsing on ice in cardiac arrest – 80% of league is vaccinated."

"Pedro Obiang: 29-year-old professional footballer suffers myocarditis after Covid-19 vaccines, possible end of career."

Newscaster: "You might be wondering how someone in such great shape could suffer cardiac arrest." "It's a rare thing that happens."

"Got two heart attacks in a few hours."

"A player suffered a double cardiac arrest!"

"Emil Palsson: Footballer collapses from cardiac arrest during game in Norway."

"Madhya Pradesh: Teen player's death due to cardiac arrest triggers concern."

"Grand Slam Champion Murphy Jensen Recovering After Suffering Sudden Cardiac Arrest While Playing Tennis."

"The story of LaPorte football's Jake West who died of sudden cardiac arrest."

"Barcelona star Sergio Aguero admitted to hospital for cardiac exam after chest pain during match."

"Three high school athletes died of sudden cardiac arrest. Their moms are fighting back."

"Young Saurashtra cricketer, Avi Barot, dies after suffering cardiac arrest."

"Runner in Bilbao half-marathon suffers three cardiac arrests."

"Soccer player goes into cardiac arrest before Saint-James vs Avranches match."

"Cardiac arrest on the track: The Colverde athlete is still serious, saved by the defibrillator."

"Sad news from Belgium: 19-year-old player dies surprisingly of cardiac arrest."

Morgan Freeman: *"I'm not a doctor, but I trust science. I'm told that for some reason, some people trust me. So, here I am to say, I trust science, and I got the vaccine. If you trust me, you'll get the vaccine."*

The next video is of a girl in an automobile. She is having a seizure. She can barely talk, but she manages to get a few words out *"Please help me, take out the vaccine."* The ambulance is on its way to her.

Jimmy Fallen: *"The good thing is, the vaccines are being rolled out. And you're on the list."*

Ricky Gervais: *"I can't wait to get the shot; I would fight an old lady. I would be happy to grab the needle out of her arm."*

Another video shows a woman in bed shaking. Her husband is trying to get her to breathe. But all she can do is moan. Her husband is rubbing her chest saying *"Breathe."* He asks if she can talk to him, but all she can do is shake and moan, just trying to breathe.

Keeping up with Corona, The Daily Distance: *"So, to keep the virus from taking hold, we need to get as many people, as quickly as possible, to get the shot."*

In this video, there is a young child in a woman's arms. She is saying, *"Breathe baby, breathe,"* but he stares across the room. She is wiping his face, trying to get him to breathe. Meanwhile, possibly his mother, is watching what is going on, and she is sobbing. It sounds like a priest may be in the background doing the last rites for the boy.

Unicef speaker: *"There are still nearly 20 million children around the world that are not getting the routine vaccines they need to be safe. So, please don't wait. Vaccinate yourself. Vaccinate your children."*

The next video is of a girl in bed. Laying on her side. She is uncontrollably shaking. She has no control over her arms, and she can't walk. She says, *"I've been hiding, not showing what this has done to me. But I am done hiding, and I'm done being scared. There are several stories like mine. The same doctors that told us that this was safe are the same doctors brushing us off as if it doesn't matter. It is now time that we are heard, seen, and believed."*

Fauci: *"The younger kids are vulnerable; you don't want to be putting something into younger children until you know it's safe and effective. So we know we are good to go from 12 – 15, so now we are going to go 12 - 9, 9 – 6, 6 to 2 years, and 6 months to 2 years."*

Tucker Carlson: *"More people, according to VAERS, have died after getting the shot in four months, during the single vaccination campaign, than from all other vaccines combined for more than a decade and a half."*

Elton John: *"The more people of society that get vaccinated, the more chance there is of eradicating this national Covid pandemic. It's really important to know that the vaccines have all been through and met the necessary safety and quality standard."*

The next video is of a mother in her car saying, *"This is for all of you clowns out there that think you have to take the shot. Don't take it! I'll tell you why. As a grieving mother, I'm going to tell you why. My daughter got the shot yesterday and now she is dead. She took that Pfizer vaccine and now she is dead. They couldn't even revive her. I'm begging you people, don't take it. They're killing us."*

Another lady tells how she got the shot, had problems, went to the doctor and the doctor told her to get used to being handicapped.

The next lady had such a bad reaction to the shot that she was afraid she would never be able to just get up to go to the bathroom.

Newscaster: *"Forty-six percent of all the deaths that happen from vaccines, for the last 31 years, happened in the last three months with these Covid vaccines."*

The next lady tells how she has lost her ability to talk.

Newscaster: *"The mother and grandmother said she was healthy before she got the shot, and that her sudden death came as a shock."*

A young man is laying in a hospital bed. He says, *"I am in the hospital with heart complications from the Covid-19 vaccination."*

Newscaster: *"The CDC confirmed higher than normal cases of heart inflammation in 16 to 24-year-olds."*

"Football player dead just hours after getting the vaccine."

"Loved ones say the 17-year old's heart stopped, suddenly collapsing."

"There is a second player that has collapsed. This is very unusual.

"This is something that no one has ever seen before. There is some evidence that there is some reaction to Covid."

A mother: *"My son is dead because he took the vaccine. They are lying, they are lying, they are lying."*

A mother and daughter in the courtroom: *"We are pro vaccines and pro science, so we agreed to let Mattie volunteer into the trial."*

"Why is social media so intent on censoring it? No one is letting anyone know. No mainstream media. Nothing. You have to dig and dig and dig to find anything, and then even then, you are called crazy."

Newscaster: *"Last week there were more deaths in America from the Covid vaccine, than from Covid itself."*

Newscaster: *"Breaking news from the FDA which just approved the emergency use of the Pfizer vaccine for children 5 to 11. By the end of the year, Dr. Fauci believes that there will be a vaccine available for kids as young as 6 months."*

Newscaster: *"That means that millions of young children will get their first dose, right now."*

Mother: *"We just want you to believe this is real. We are real people experiencing these side effects."*

Dr. Michael Yeadon: *"It's a crazy thing to vaccinate them with something that is 50 times more likely to kill them than the virus itself."*

Fauci: *"What is the problem? Get over it!"*

"Come on people. Just get the shot!"

And now that's become the new norm with these death shots. They're killing us. Then there's what's called the third and final phase that we've yet to see, and what Dr. Zelenko was talking about. That is the Long-Term Death phase, where we will see the true, long-term fallout over these death shots in a couple years. And if you think that won't happen, then let's listen to our second example of a medical expert admitting that Mass Genocide is really coming very soon from the Covid death shots.

Dr. Charles Hoffe: mRNA vaccines will kill most people through heart failure, 62% already have microscopic blood clots

His name is **Dr. Charles Hoffe.** He speaks with another panel of doctors who are saying that the Long-Term Death count that Dr. Zelenko is talking about, really is coming fast and here's how it's going to happen.

Dr. Charles Hoffe: *"The concern is that these vessels are now permanently damaged in a person's lungs. When the heart tries to pump blood through all those damaged vessels, there's increased resistance trying to pump the blood to those lungs. So, those people are going to develop something called 'pulmonary artery hypertension,' or high blood pressure in their lungs. And the concern with that is that those people will probably all develop the right-sided heart failure within three years and die."*

So, it's coming whether people realize it or not. And again, for a more detailed study on this horrible reality of the Covid death shots, get our documentary, **The Great Covid Deception.**

But now let's get back to our legal expert, Todd Callender, and the question we posed. Based on the evidence, it really would appear that, when you put it to the test, and be that Berean, that his statement is really true, *"Mass Genocide is coming with these Covid shots that have been coordinated by Global entities."* Now let's go on to his next statement and see what else Todd shares in The Corona Investigative Committee Interview.

Dr. Reiner Fuellmich: *"I saw a little video clip in which you were interviewed, I forget who it was that interviewed you, but you told them about incredible, or should I say, excess mortality, and I don't know what caused this excess mortality, but it must have something to do with this so-called vaccination, of course. It may be part of the nanoparticles or maybe the spike protein, I don't know. What do you know?"*

Todd Callender: *"Yes, I do know. It's not only a question. We have figured this out. So, the lipid nanoparticles are like little bombers, and they are carrying payloads. These payloads are lipid nucleotides, messenger mRNA and synthetic DNA's. Those are the payloads of these little bombers. In order to slip those little bombers past the human's natural immunity, they had to disarm people's natural immunity.*

They used three different HIV proteins, the GP120, the AD5, as an additive, and the PP14. Those three proteins were injected into the humans for the purpose of allowing the lipid nanoparticle bombers to go into the cells, deliver those payloads, and then create synthetic DNA, the recombinant mRNA and the recombinant DNA. We know all of that. We also know what the pathogens are in at least some of the shots, because it's in their past. What is particularly alarming, in terms of all of these numbers of excess mortality and morbidity, is that the people that put these three HIV proteins into the shots disarmed people's natural immunity, gave them vaccine-induced AIDS, and they didn't give them anything to reverse it.

So, now what you are seeing in terms of all causes of morbidity and mortality. The numbers that I got came out of the U.S. Department of Defense's own database called DMET (The Depart of Medical Educational and Training database) So, again going back to my lawsuit against the DoD, I called several acquaintances who testified in both our temporary restraining order and in our NAR preliminary injunction, one of whom was Dr. Teresa Long. You might have seen her and some other notable ones, including Dr. McCullough. We have come to understand all of this with a group of medical experts and scientists, who have come to our aid and understanding. All of this that I am telling you I can backup with evidence, and I will be happy to do that.

What is even more concerning, when you see a 1,100 percent increase in all causes of morbidity and mortality, that means something systemic has caused this problem. So, you would see an abnormal increase of all causes, cancer, heart issues, inflammation issues, blood clotting, and I can actually send you what that looks like to add proof of a mortality basis. When you see all of them rising to 100's of percentiles in a class of people who are physically fit from 18 to 45, they are all military people, there is only one cause for this, and that is the destruction of their immune system. So, that is the vaccine-induced auto-immune deficiency syndrome. We know this now. In fact, it's in the signs all around. The Israeli's, they are ahead of everybody else. They already published papers on this. Everybody knows this. The short answer to this whole thing is that everybody that got the shot was given some form or level of AIDS."

Whoa! Now, wait a second there. "Everybody that got these shots was given some form or level of AIDS?" Could that be true as well? Well, again, let's put it to the test. Let's be those Bereans. Not only do these shots "not" cure Covid as a traditional vaccine is supposed to do, but neither do they prevent it, let alone stop the spread of it, and that's all over the news.

What you will see, when you examine the facts, is that as crazy as it sounds, these vaccines not only "don't" cure Covid, but rather, they actually are designed, just like Todd Callender said, to "destroy people's immune systems," which by the way is the definition of AIDS. And this is why there is such a "high morbidity rate with these shots." In other words, this is why so many people are dying, and will continue to die from them. They destroy your immune system by giving you AIDS.

That means, any preexisting condition you might have, or any genetic leaning towards something, like what Todd mentioned there, such as cancer, heart complications, etc., are going to spike like crazy and come back like wildfire, because these people that got these shots have no immune system left in them to fight anything off. But could this be true? Unfortunately, yes, and Todd's not the only one sounding the alarm on this. Watch this.

Narrator: *"Let's take a little stroll down memory lane, shall we? The year was 2020 and the human race was just entering into the year of a deadly pandemic. The despair that overcame families, they cancelled their holiday festivities, was balanced by a fresh feeling of hope as the miracle of science just introduced the world's first Coronavirus vaccine. But even miracles come with their own little bugs to work out. The Covid vaccine came with its very specific bug of its own. The kind of bug that causes AIDS."*

Newspaper clipping: *"Australia Scraps Covid-19 vaccine that produced HIV false positives."*

Narrator: *"Just weeks before Christmas, the Australian Government made the decision to trash 51 million doses of the Covid vaccine after trial participants returned false positive HIV test results. They say that the reason for this decision has nothing to do with safety and everything to do with upholding the public's confidence in the new treatment. You see, much of the world in its selective state of amnesia, have forgotten the small details about the early pandemic vaccine rollout. But I haven't!"*

Newspaper clipping: *"Researcher Warns Some Covid-19 Vaccines Could Increase Risk of HIV Infection."*

Newspaper clipping: *"Use of Adenovirus Type-5 Vectored Vaccines: A Cautionary Tale."*

"I remember October 2020, when researchers expressed concern that the Covid vaccine could increase the risk of HIV infection, ultimately leading to an increase in infections as vaccines rolled out to volatile populations around the world. I remember all the way back in April 2020, when Luc Montagnier, world-renowned biologist, and winner of the 2008 Nobel Prize for his discovery of HIV, who warned the world that the Novel Coronavirus was not of natural origin and that it was manipulated to include sequences from the HIV virus.

Now fast forward three years to the present, 2022. Billions of these vaccines have been administered across the globe. That feeling of hope is thick in the air once again. And on a completely unrelated note, everyone has AIDS.

Newspaper clipping: *"HIV now infects more heterosexual people than gay or bisexual men – we need a new strategy."*

Newspaper clipping: *"Highly virulent HIV variant found circulating in Europe."*

Headlines read for the first time in over a decade, HIV now infects more heterosexual than gay or bisexual men, and a highly virulent HIV is circulating in Europe. And even Prince Harry in England, is urging everyone to know their status and get tested for HIV. Now, I'm not claiming that any of these events are linked because if this pandemic has taught me anything, it's that confirmation is real, and correlation does not equal causation. So, there is definitely no connection between any of this and the fact that just two weeks ago, Moderna wants their clinical trial for an HIV vaccine that uses mRNA technology. And its definitely just coincidence that Luc Montagnier, that highly regarded biologist who warned of the dangers of the HIV splice in the Novel Coronavirus, died on Tuesday."

Yeah, I'm sure that was by chance. No! These people are murderous psychopaths, and it gets worse as you go. These shots are actually destroying people's immune systems, i.e., giving them AIDS, and we are now, not so surprisingly, seeing a massive spike in all kinds of morbidity rates of various ailments and diseases skyrocketing off the charts. Why? Because they have got AIDS now, and they can't fight off anything! They have no immune system left!

And just like Todd Callender said, Israel is already ahead of the curve admitting this. **"FDA report finds all-cause mortality higher among vaccinated,"** and that's from the Israel National News.

FDA report finds all-cause mortality higher among vaccinated

FDA report shows Pfizer's clinical trials found 24% higher all-cause mortality rate among the vaccinated compared to placebo group. Report emphasizes that "None of the deaths were considered related to vaccination."

And other studies show **"COVID-19 Vaccines INCREASE Deaths and Hospitalizations from COVID-19 Based on Analysis of Most-Vaccinated Countries."**

And talk about sick, "**Covid Death Shot: 1000% Increase in Vaccine Deaths & Injuries Among Children Post-Covid Vaccination.**" And again, this is happening because these people who got the shots no longer have an immune system, i.e., they now have AIDS, and so they can't fight off any diseases. This is why cancer rates, heart attacks, blood disorders, you name it, have gone off the chart. In fact, here's another doctor, Dr. Elizabeth Eads, admitting that just cancer rates alone have gone up 2,000% from the Covid shots.

Greg Hunter, USA Watchdog Reports:
"Luc Montagnier won a Nobel Prize for his groundbreaking work on HIV in 2008. He died just a couple of months ago, but the last thing he tweeted was that the double-vaxed and boosted, should check themselves for HIV. That was verbatim what he said. And here we have, low and behold, I just want you to listen to this. This is an expose from the U.K. 'While we are being distracted by Russia, the Ukraine, the U.K., the government silently published data confirming the triple-vaccinated are just weeks away from developing 'Acquired Immune Deficiency Syndrome.' Let that sink in. 'Acquired Immune Deficiency Syndrome.' AIDS!

And one of the people I thought about when I saw this among the frontline doctors was Dr. Elizabeth Eads. Dr. Eads, thank you for joining us today

on USA Watchdog. Are you starting to now see acquired immune deficiency syndrome from people who have been vaxed?"

Dr. Elizabeth Eads: *"Well thanks for having me today, Greg, and, yes, we are seeing vaccine-related acquired immune deficiency in the hospitals now from the triple-vaxed."*

Greg Hunter: *"Now, this is not some small, I mean Luc Montagnier, this was one of his last tweets that he put out, that you should get tested for HIV or acquired immune deficiency syndrome. This is awful. You can't take a pill and get rid of it, right? This is a vax injury, right?"*

Dr. Elizabeth Eads: *"This is a vax injury, and we're not really certain how to treat this. We're kind of throwing the kitchen sink at it. We are throwing antiretrovirals at it. We are throwing Interferon at it, Ivermectin, hydroxychloroquine, anti-parasitics, that are in studies right now. We are trying to use everything we can think of to boost up the CD4 and CD8 T-cells, and reverse this collapse, this calamity, of immune collapse. It's very stunning.*

Greg Hunter: *"You were talking in past interviews and said, listen, this is how the math goes. First shot, generally speaking, you lose 20 percent and then you lose a bigger percent with the booster. Even Dr. Michael Yeadon, before the very first shot was given, they said whatever you do, don't get the booster, whatever you do. You have a special name for the booster. You are seeing it in action. The people who are double-vaxed and boosted, your term is the kill shot. Am I correct? Did I get that right?"*

Dr. Elizabeth Eads: *"The kill shot, the money ball, whatever you want to call it. It is just devastating to the immune system. And I will tell you why it is devastating. If you look at the Stanford Study, I'm just going to read a couple sentences from the Stanford Study to you. 'The Spike protein in the Covid-19 vaccines that everyone is talking about is called the Lentivirus. The Lenti contains a combination of HIV types 1-3 SRV-1which is AIDS, MERS, and SARS. In the Stanford Study, the best-known Lentivirus is the human immune deficiency pathogen, which causes AIDS. This is why you* *are seeing auto-immune and neuro-degenerative decline after Covid-19 vaccine and especially the booster. This is a condition known as Crion and the mRNA from the Lentivirus cocktail is inserted into the DNA of human cells through an invasive procedure, injection, and permanently changes the genome of the cell.*

That is why this is terrifying to us in the medical community, because we just don't know how to attack."

Greg Hunter: *"Wait a minute. A lot of people have a hard time of putting their heads around this. That you got acquired immune deficiency syndrome because it was put into the vaccine. (The injections, the inoculations) Is that what you are telling me?"*

Dr. Elizabeth Eads: *"That is exactly what I am telling you. That is what this spike Lentivirus is. It is made up of HIV and AIDS along with SARS and MERS. That is why the vaccinated and boosted are so sick. That's why they dominate the hospitalization regarding Covid illness right now as well."*

Greg Hunter: *"When people find out this little piece of information, they are going to be angry. You don't have to draw a big picture. Oh yeah, the vaccines that you got, shot one, shot two and the boosters, you now have acquired immune deficiency syndrome. You have now got AIDS. How do you feel? People are going to be upset, are they not? You could die from somebody coughing on you."*

Dr. Elizabeth Eads: *"Correct. And what that does is it actually drops the CD4 and the CD8 counts which are integral in fighting off infection. And now some pretty wise physicians are checking those CD-4's, CD-8's T-cell counts, and white cells counts and doing the purple smears, looking for this. Along with the D-Dimer tests, looking for the clots. So, we are seeing it, we are recognizing it, and now we are trying to aggressively treat for opportunistic infections. And those infections could be pneumonia, could be a fungal infection, herpes, salmonella, TB, mycobacterium. There are a number of things that could happen when you* *have no CD-8, no CD-4 cells. You can't even keep cancer cells in check. You are going to have a rise in cancer, such as lung cancer, liver cancer, Hodgkin's disease, anal cancer, cervical cancer, skin cancer, testicular cancer, etc. Let me tell you, Dr. Ryan Paul is a very prominent pathologist, and he's receiving slides from all over the country of unusual cancers, and he has seen a 2000 percent rise in cancer since the onset of these Covid shots."*

Wow! Let that sink in for a little bit. But that's just cancer. There's also a massive increase of other health-related illnesses and disease spikes all over the world since the Covid shots were rolled out. It's almost like people's immune systems have been destroyed. Go figure.

In fact, Dr. Eads went on to say, *"Millions will get AIDS from the Covid Vaccine by the fall,"* which means even more deaths, because they have no immune system. Is this crazy or what? How sick are these people? As you can see, once you examine the facts, it really does appear that Todd Callender was right in his statement. People really are being given AIDS on purpose with these Covid vaccines, and it really is causing a massive spike in morbidity rates of all kinds of health-related issues. This is part of the reason why so many people are dying.

Now let's go back to Todd's next statement and see what else he says in the next segment of The Corona Investigative Committee Interview.

Todd Callender: *"The auto-immune deficiency syndrome, the ones that got the one shot, it seems that they have about 30 percent of their natural immunity destroyed. By the time they have the three shots their immunity is completely gone. We are seeing that with our doctors, the experts, in their practices, including on base and off base, the real epidemic is now. I happen to be in the morbidity business. I'm a CEO in a large insurance group and we underwrite morbidity risks. Specifically, disability, accidents, health. Based on what it is we are seeing, the rates right now for excess mortality, 84 percent, excess every other kind, 1100 percent and* *we are expecting a 5,000 or so percent increase in excess mortality for this year. An enormous number.*

I don't think that it is by coincidence, by the way, that Moderna has just now received licenses for their emergency use authorization HIV vaccine. So, they gave everybody AIDS, and now here is your salvation, which seems to be a multiple-dose vaccine."

What? So, they gave people AIDS with this vaccine, and now they just so happen to come out with an AIDS vaccine? Isn't that convenient! But is this true? Well, again, let's put it to the test. Let's be those Bereans. It just so happens when all this was coming out, about these shots giving people AIDS and cancer, among other diseases, and that they're going through the roof, guess who's coming out with vaccines for both?

That's right folks, the same entities making the vaccines! Shocker! In fact, as you can see here:

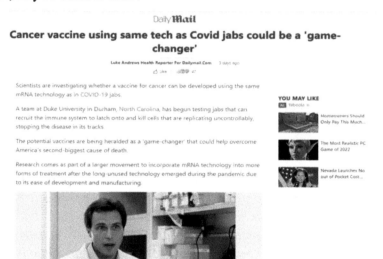

"Cancer vaccine using same tech as Covid jabs could be a game-changer." as reported in the UK. And even here in the U.S.

"Promising cancer vaccine in the works utilizing similar mRNA technology that combats COVID."

promising-cancer-vaccine-utilizing-similar-mrna-technology-combats-covid-duke-researchers

HEALTH · Published April 18, 2022 3:06am EDT

Promising cancer vaccine in the works utilizing similar mRNA technology that combats COVID: Duke researchers

Duke researchers find potential in a cancer vaccine based on the same messenger RNA, or mRNA, technology used by COVID-19 vaccines

By Shiv Sudhakar | Fox News

White House press secretary Jen Psaki put a stop to questions Friday about whether

So, if you're sick and tired of getting cancer or all the other plethora of diseases and ailments, that you now get from taking the Covid shot, because you now have no immune system left, i.e., you have AIDS, hey no worries, these same companies have come out with an AIDS vaccine as well.

12News Reports: *"Moderna has developed a new mRNA vaccine to prevent HIV and AIDS with clinical trials beginning soon."*

Yup, I'm sure that's a big ol' coinkydink! Are you kidding me? These guys are liars, and again, as we saw in our previous study *"**The Great Covid Deception**,"* these Covid shots are not only a massive killing machine, creating skyrocketing death rates all over the world, but they are also a massive money-making scheme because now the people who got the shots have to keep going back to the supplier to get more shots just to stay alive, as this Doctor admits.

This health practitioner is not ready to share her identity at this time but her presented information is invaluable.

Health Practitioner: *"I am a natural doctor, and I have 1600 patients; many are vaccinated. Just to give you a little back story of my credibility. What I have seen so far and what I have learned is all information from medical physicians, natural physicians, and also immunization virology doctors and then also nurses. So, what I am about to share with you is the first vaccine, then the second vaccine and then the booster and what it does to your body.*

The first vaccine, as it goes into your body, has a small amount of saline, with a whole bunch of ingredients that are very catastrophic to your cellular system. What that does to your immune system, which is your bone marrow, your thymus gland, your spleen, and all other systems associated with your immune system, it decreases your ability to produce white blood cells by 50 percent from your first vaccine.

Then eight weeks later your white blood cell reproductive system, your ability to produce white blood cells is 8 weeks. That is why they set it up eight weeks later, to hit it up again. So, you hit the white blood ability while it is down. Now, they decrease the saline in the second and increase the harmful ingredients, so now you have a shift in ingredients. And then what they do with the second dose, it attacks your ability to produce white blood cells by an additional 25 percent. So, now you only have the ability to produce white blood cells functioning at 25 percent. You just wiped-out 75 percent of your military and the ability to make that military.

So, now what they do is set in the booster. The booster has 81 strands of foreign bacteria that your cells have never come across. You don't have the antibodies to fight it, you only have 25 percent of your white blood cells in production to be able to fight it. So, it's a losing battle. Now what begins to happen is you start to get chronic inflammation that goes to the area that you had predisposition. So, if you are someone that has gut health issues, that is the area that it will focus on. You are going to have inflammation in the gut. If it's respiratory, you have a tumor or cancer or if you have endometriosis or a skin condition, whatever it is, it will inflame that area because now the body has hit the sympathetic nervous system, and the body is in a chronic inflammatory state with a low immunity and low immunity response.

Then you get your second booster. What the second booster has in it is eight strands of HIV, and what that does is it completely shuts off the ability to make white blood cells (you can google what that disease is). It is HIV. Now we have people walking around with no immune system, no ability to make an immune system, 81 strands of foreign bacteria and eight strands of foreign HIV along with all the other harmful ingredients. And then they remove all the saline from the first and second booster.

Now to make matters worse during this process, 20-30 percent of the population is going to die every single series of this process, and there are four series. They have three more boosters that are coming out, and the reason why is because once they make you so that your immune system cannot make white blood cells anymore, you become dependent on the boosters to survive just like someone becomes dependent on insulin. Big Pharma is looking for people that will either die off to protect our population control, and those that don't die off, they will have reoccurring customers for life, with the boosters, so that they will be able to maintain the income and collect the money back for all the funding that they put in to make these vaccines in the first place.

So, I hope this was helpful and you listened to this properly, and I hope you take the time to do your own critical thinking and give it two or three years. Every single animal that participated in this study had a 100 percent death rate."

And now it's coming our way. Again, these are psychopathic murderers, as well as greedy evil rotten people. They figured out a way to destroy our immune system, so we'd always have to go back to them for another shot just to stay alive. How is that any different than a drug dealer that gets somebody hooked on drugs? It's not! Now they have a customer for life too! Pretty slick, isn't it? It's the same ol' technique, only applied to the biggest drug dealer of them all, Big Pharma.

But as you can see, as wild as it sounded at first, once you put it to the test, it really does appear to be true. "Everybody that got these shots was given some form or level of AIDS," and now the same entities, "have just come out with an AIDS vaccine." Go figure!

Chapter Three

The Trigger of Human 2.0

Now hold on to your seatbelt because here's where it gets incredibly worse. We are about to enter the proverbial Twilight Zone. Let's go back to another piece of information Todd shares in The Corona Investigative Committee Interview.

Todd Callender: *"Almost worse than that, and again going back to me standing on the shoulders of these experts, I've figured out that there is this electromagnetic connection to all of this. You would have seen during the lockdown period for almost two years, at least here in the United States and several other countries, that there was a massive installation of 5G networks. They were put in every single public school in the United States, and most private ones, brand new 5G rates from the 2 to 300 GHz range Each one of those signals does different things. In fact, they can mimic the very same kind of symptomology as Covid. For instance, Halloween night of 2019, Wuhan was the first city in the world to go 5G. They turned on 10,000 transmitters.*

Within the coming days, they had this massive problem where the Chinese were literally falling over dead, which is not exactly the same symptomology as the normal Covid, with people standing on the street and falling over dead. It turns out that a 60 GHz signal, which is a 5G signal, is actually capable of separating oxygen from the nitrogen. So, some people, according to our experts, literally standing on the street, and through the targeting device known as their cell phone, were able to rip the oxygen from the nitrogen, and with the people breathing only the nitrogen and not getting the oxygen, would literally fall over dead. 5G is like a butcher's knife. It's a dual use item. You can use it to communicate, and, at the same time, you can use it to kill."

Okay, now that was a mouthful! So, on top of everything we've seen so far, the next thing shared in this interview, is that there was also an "electromagnetic component" built into this Covid Plandemic, as well as the solution called the Covid vaccines. This involved the installation of 5G technology that was installed en masse around the world at the same time Covid- 19 was being released upon the planet. It was being put in schools across America as well as in Wuhan, China, where the outbreak is reportedly to have first started, with people dropping dead on the street. And it's a dangerous technology with a "dual purpose." You can "use it to communicate or use it to kill."

Is this true? Talk about science fiction. Well, again, let's put it to the test. Time to be a Berean again. First, let's educate ourselves on this technology called 5G. What's it all about? Let's take a look.

NBC News Reports: *"4G is the mobile network used around the world to make calls and send messages and surf the web. Now there are plans for 4G to be replaced by, you guessed it, 5G. A new, faster network that has the potential to transform the internet. 5G is a software defined network, that means, while it won't replace cables entirely, it could replace the need for them, by largely operating on the cloud instead. This means you will have a 100 times better capacity than 4G, which will dramatically improve internet speed.*

For example, to download a two-hour film on 3G it would take about 26 hours. On 4G you would be waiting 6 minutes. And on 5G you would be able to watch your film in 3.6 seconds. But it's not just internet capacity that will be upgraded; response time will also be much faster. The 4G network responds to our command in just under 50 milliseconds, but with 5G it will take 1 millisecond, 400 times faster than a blink of the eye. Smart phone users will enjoy a more streamlined experience. In a world that is becoming increasingly more dependent just to function, a reduction in time delay is critical. Some experts predict that by 2025 nearly half of all mobile connections in the U.S. will be 5G, a greater percentage than any other country or region."

You might be thinking, "Well, so what? What's the big deal about having faster internet downloads, and speeds, and times? I could care less about 5G." Well, you should care, because this technology will allow the Global Elites to create, for the very first time, what's called IOT or the Internet of Things, where all products and all people can be connected to a Global Matrix! It will have the ability to connect with your so-called Smart Home, with your Smart Car, with your Smart Office, your Smart Watch, Smart Phone and all your other Smart Devices including your Smart Appliances, even Smart Shoes. It monitors you, your family, your health, and everyone's every move! Isn't that smart?

The installation of 5G technology around the world allows these Global Elites to literally connect every single product and every single person on the face of the earth, all at the same time, continuously, in a non-stop monitoring system that they tell us will lead to a life beyond our wildest dreams! In fact, here's one of their promotional videos showing us just what kind of utopia they're building for us, and we should be grateful for, with 5G.

Life Simplified with Cloud-based Automation

Mom and dad have been out riding their bikes. When they come home, the sensor on the side of their house automatically opens the garage door. They park their bikes in the garage and go into the kitchen. It is now 7:00 AM. The oven automatically comes on, and she gets a message on her phone that the oven is pre-heating to 350 degrees. It will be ready in 5:42 minutes. The next message she gets is a question. "Add sensor with open door alerts? Yes or No?" She walks to the refrigerator, and she gets a notification on her phone that a door has been opened. The door that was opened was the bathroom door. Her husband has come in to refresh himself. The notification on the phone says, "Room occupied, door locked." The next message tells her, "Occupied: Dad – Shower: 106 degrees."

One of their kids is in the other bathroom and is brushing her hair. The message reads, "Room occupied – Lights on." When the little girl leaves the room, the message reads, "Lights off." Now we go back to the kitchen. The refrigerator takes an inventory and proceeds to send the message that they have lettuce, tomatoes, and orange juice, but eggs are out of stock. By this time there is music playing all through the house. The little girl goes into her brother's bedroom and hits him with a pillow to get him up to start his day. While the mother is still in the kitchen, she picks up her phone to increase the volume of the stereo in her son's bedroom. That gets him up out of bed, dressed and down to the kitchen to eat breakfast.

As dad is finishing up his breakfast, ready to go to work, another notification comes on the phone. "Vehicle Diagnostics, + tires, + oil, + gas/below ¼ tank, + fluids." A notification comes on the phone to tell him that the car needs more gas and "to avoid delay, leave in 3 minutes." He finishes his breakfast and goes out to the car. He pushes the button to start the car and the message comes on saying, "Toxic fumes, open garage door."

Mom and the kids are heading off to school, but the son goes back to the refrigerator to get a container of juice. The message is sent, "The refrigerator door is open." When he looks at his phone, he sees that the door didn't close completely when he shut it, so he turns around to push the door shut. When they leave the house, a notification comes on saying, "Current occupants: 0, Energy Saving Mode." And the thermostat goes up to 81 degrees.

Now a notification comes on that says, "Dad at work, deactivate office." But as he walks through the door it changes to read, "Dad at work, activate office. Wake up computer. Open shades." A few minutes later,

"9:45 AM Design Meeting. +Participants – Present, + Conference Room 1 – Booked, + Move to Conference Room 2." That message has been sent to dad, and he proceeds on to Conference Room 2.

As mom is taking the kids to school a message comes on advising her that the speed limit is 35 mph. Her speed is 37 mph. After dropping off the kids, a notification tells her, "Son and daughter are in class." She proceeds to speak to her phone, "Order two smoothies at the restaurant for my 1:00 meeting." She gets the confirmation back, "Order Placed."

While everyone is gone, a person comes up to their front door. He holds a bar code up to the sensor on the porch and the notification reads, "+ Sprinkler repair man, +1:30 PM appointment, +Wi-Fi access required." The message pops up on dad's phone, and he presses "Yes" to allow the sprinkler repair man to proceed. "Access is granted." Suddenly, a notification is sent saying, "Flood water present." "Toxic fumes." This is to be taken care of. The sensors are already getting things prepared at home, for the end of the day, and what's for dinner? The notification says, "Dinner Recipe: Burritos, + Tortillas, + Avocados, + Beans, + Rice/out of stock." Once again, the mom looks at her phone, and the notification reminds her, "Rice and eggs are out of stock."

When she reaches the restaurant for her meeting, a notification is sent to the waiter that they are there and to bring the smoothies to the table. "Order delivered, process payment." Later that evening, dad and son are outside in the yard. Notification comes on stating, "Soccer Practice Statistics: + 22-29 Session, + 38/47 Goals, + 80.9% Accuracy, + 21.4 MP Average Shooting Speed. Email statistics. Lawn Sprinklers: + 5:00 PM, + Forecast: No Rain, + Lawn: Occupied – Delay, Sprinklers off."

They also have a garden in the backyard. And there is a notification about it as well. "Soil moisture: 0.2. Start irrigation." As mom is getting the table ready for dinner there is a notification that someone is at the door. With the visitor identification sensor, the people at the door are approved guests. They are grandma and grandpa. "Unlock the door." Everyone runs to greet them. They have a wonderful meal of burritos and a lovely

evening, but then it's time for them to go home. Notifications are coming on that read, "Room unoccupied, lights on, lights off, 8:00 PM, lock doors."

Wow! Who wouldn't want to live in that paradise, huh? Yeah, can you say a rat in a cage? I don't want to live like that, like a rat, monitored in a cage 24/7, wherever I go non-stop! Are you kidding me? No thank you! But this is what the installation of 5G will allow these Global Elites to do. Every so-called Smart device and every single person on the whole planet is going to be connected to this Internet of Things, or IOT. They pitch it as building a life of convenience, when in reality, it will lead to a life of slavery and constant monitoring!

Was this system really installed in schools across America, and other places at the same time Covid-19 was being spread around? Yes, as you can see here!

"5G Biometrics Systems Being Covertly Installed in Schools During Coronavirus Lockdowns." Notice the date there, April 22, 2020, right after the lockdown. In fact, this reporter shares the same suspicions I have.

MOM Show Reports: *"5G, hundreds of respected scientists sound the alarm about health affects as 5G networks go up nationwide. A little sidenote here. When did they go up? During lockdown. March of 2020. Fauci and Gates said, 'Stay home, stay safe.' Are you kidding me? They wanted us dead for years. So, I knew there was something going on behind closed 'House' doors, and that's when this journey began.*

Last year we put up at least a dozen videos talking about what I believe is really going on behind the scenes with Bill Gates and his cohorts putting up 5G, deadly radiation, death towers around the globe. You can find this article in the show notes. It's from Michael Snyder, written on May 19, 2019, and here's what he wrote. 'Even though many in the scientific community are loudly warning of the potential health effects that 5G technology would have on the general population, Verizon and AT&T are starting to put up their 5G networks. Their total number of cellphones exceed the number of the entire population of the world.

These cellphone companies are making a crazy amount of money providing service to all of those phones. 5G will transform the way our citizens work, learn, communicate, and travel. Sounds awesome, right? In order to achieve such vastly superior performance, 5G networks will use technology that is completely different than 4G networks. 5G waves are ultra-high frequencies and ultra-high intensity.

So, although those cell towers will be much, much smaller, they will also need to be much, much closer together than ever before. According to CBS News, it is estimated that the big cell phone companies will be putting up at least 300,000 of these small towers and has been projected that it will cost hundreds of billions of dollars to fully set up this 5G network nationwide. Needless to say, there is a tremendous amount of money at stake. And the big cell phone companies are trying very hard to assure you that their 5G technology is completely safe, but is it?

Today there is a growing body of scientific evidence that indicates that the electromagnetic radiation that we are constantly being bombarded with is not good for us. Cancer risks, genetic damages, functional changes of the reproductive system, and neurological disorders are some of the health risks and, remember, because the 5G towers are going to be so powerful and so close together, it will be essentially like living in a closed radiation chamber 24 hours a day. What's further disturbing about 5G radiation is how the human body responds to and processes it.

A scientist from the Hebrew University of Jerusalem discovered as part of a recent investigation that human skin acts as a type of receptor for 5G radiation.' I will read it again, this scientist from the Hebrew University of Jerusalem discovered as part of a recent investigation that human skin acts as a type of receptor for 5G radiation, drawing it in like an antenna. 'No studies have been done on the health effects of our new ultra-powerful 5G technology. Unfortunately, there are no organized opposition and there are 5G networks going up all over the country right now as I speak. I have to note that the person who is a major player behind the 5G Networks going up around this globe is none other than Bill Gates.'

Check this out. I found out a little over a year ago that Bill Gates bought 5.3 million shares in Crown Castle. Crown Castle is the largest provider of shared U.S. Communications Infrastructure. Guess what? Crown Castle is the very company that put up all these death towers around the globe when Fauci and Gates told us to stay home, stay safe, so they could install these harmful, hideous, 5G towers around our globe so we wouldn't put up a stink."

So, it wasn't just that 5G technology went up during the lockdowns over the so-called Covid Plandemic crisis, but it was spearheaded by the Global Elites who did it at the exact time we couldn't and/or wouldn't put up a stink! It's called a distraction again. Pretty slick, isn't it? Same ol' pattern. But is 5G really harmful as she was alluding to? I mean, if you look at YouTube or Google, it's rare to find anything negative about 5G technology.

Well, that's why you have to go to alternative news sites and really be a Berean and discover the truth that hasn't been scrubbed by these entities. This "scrubbing" or manipulative behavior is also what we covered in another one of our documentaries called: *"Subliminal Seduction: How the Mass Media Mesmerizes the Minds of the Masses."*

Virtually all information and all media outlets around the world are controlled by a handful of Billionaire Elites who admit they are only allowing us to see and read and hear what they want us to. That's called controlling the narrative, which is a creative way of saying we're brainwashing you. But check out that documentary for more info on that. Again, if you do your homework, and be that Berean, you'll see that many people were warning about the dangers of 5G long before Covid ever hit.

From February 6, 2019, "**A global catastrophe: Radiation activist warns that 5G networks are massive health experiment.**"

It goes on to say, "The deployment of 5G constitutes an experiment on humanity and the environment that is defined as a crime under international law." And "This could become a global catastrophe."

Did the 5G rollout in Wuhan damage the innate cellular defense cells of the population, putting the people at risk of complications and death from coronavirus?

Scientists have been sounding the alarm about the dangers of 5th generation wireless technology. Some countries have heeded the warning about wireless radiation and the harmful effects of EMFs. China, on the other hand, has completely ignored all warnings and has proceeded to unleash 5G faster than any other nation. In fact, China rolled out 5G in the province of Wuhan in October 2019. Just two months later, the city became afflicted by a new kind of coronavirus named Covid-19. How did a formerly benign class of virus become so opportunistic in such a short amount of time? Why is the death rate so high at the epicenter of the outbreak?

And this article shared way back in the day, some three years ago, **"5G Is Coming, And with it Potentially Calamitous Health Risks."**

prepforthat.com/5g-health-risks/

Alternative Health   Prepper News

5G Is Coming, And With It Potentially Calamitous Health Risks

3 years ago Meredith Iager

f Share This   Share This

You want fast wireless service. Enhanced wireless data speeds are premium services that stand to make Wireless companies billions (and already do). The newest technological enhancement to improved wireless data speeds is 5G. The installation of 5G cell towers is not only going to improve speed, but it is also likely to have a detrimental effect on our public health. Wireless companies have already installed up

Which then goes on to list just a few of those proposed health risks:

- Different Cancers
- Reproductive Problems, Infertility
- Suppressed Immune System Function
- Neurological Problems
- Headaches/Migraines
- Effects on Eyes, Heart, Lungs, Head – Essentially your entire body is affected
- Single & Double DNA Strand Breaks
- Oxidative Damage
- Stress of Proteins
- Disruption to Brain for Glucose Metabolism
- Reduces Melatonin in the Brain
- Brain Barrier Permeability (Could result in brain bleeds, Stroke)
- Cell Metabolism Disruption

In fact, here's some words of warning from various medical experts, including some of their governmental hearings over what kind of dangers 5G technology really is going to expose us to.

Narrator: *"Across the country and around the world, awareness is growing that the new generation of 5G wireless technology comes with a heavy price tag; privacy, security, public safety, property values, and, of* *course, our health. And sadly, everyone will pay, whether they use the 5G service or not. In 2018 the U.S. National Toxicology Program of the National Institute of Health completed a 30-million-dollar study to determine whether or not radio frequency radiation, the kind emitted by cell phones, Wi-Fi and cell towers, caused cancer and other health problems. The scientists who reviewed the ground-breaking study concluded that the study showed 'clear evidence of cancer, heart damage and DNA damage.' So, the issue of where to put the new 5G and other wireless antennas was a concern. Families with small children don't want them nearby. Women who are or may become pregnant shouldn't live near them. People with compromised immune systems, implant medical devices, or sensitivity to radiation should avoid them.*

Wireless companies are unhappy with the public resistance to 5G and wireless antennas. They are aware that while everyone wants convenience, no one wants trouble. You might not even know about the installation unless of course you had a meter to measure the radiation levels in your home, or you get sick. Salesmen, from the wireless industry, who will be knocking on your door to sell you this service, probably won't tell you that these antennas can be used to track your movement the minute you step out of your door. The data from your phone, your computer, video doorbells, smart refrigerator, and smart speaker, the internet of things (IOT) will be collected and used. And wireless transmissions carrying your personal data can be easily hacked.

It's important to understand what the 5G is doing and what they say it is doing. We are told on the IEEE forming document that this technology cooked your eyes like eggs in WWII. We all need to understand these are military weapons. These are assault frequencies. You garner nothing more than that. That's what you need to know. It's microwave radiation warfare, is what this is."

Senate Hearing on Bill 637

Dr. Sharon Goldberg, Internal Medicine Physician: *"Twenty-One years and my background is mostly academic, internal medicine, hospital-*

based, clinical research, and medical education."

Senator Patrick Colbeck, State of Michigan: *"I'm a certified Microsoft small business specialist. I've worked on space stations, designing the cabling system for the airlock module where I was responsible for EMI EMC analysis, which is electromagnetic interference, electromagnetic compatibility."*

Dr. Paul Heroux, Epidemiology Biostatistics and Occupational Health-McGill University: *"I teach both toxicology and health effects of electromagnetic radiation."*

Dafna Tachover, wearetheevidence.org: *"We are an organization that represents many adults, and unfortunately, many children who have become very sick from the wireless technology radiation."*

Senator Patrick Colbeck: *"There seems to be a couple of false Easter eggs being put out there right now, and I just want to make sure we dispel that right out of the gate."*

Dr. Paul Heroux: *"The effects of wireless on health, scientifically, are very, very clear."*

Senator Patrick Colbeck: *"So, it's always push back to the definition of an acceptable level of radiation. And that is what this is, by the way. This is about radiation."*

Dafna Tachover: *"Wireless radiation has biological effects, period."*

Dr. Angie Colbeck, Pediatrician: *"I have been reviewing the studies showing the impact of wireless radiation on our health and there are now thousands of studies showing the following adverse health impacts of wireless radiation: Cancer, oxidated damage, DNA damage, DNA failure."*

Dr. Paul Heroux: *"Things like memory, dizziness, anxiety, brain fog."*

Dafna Tachover: *"Headaches, cognitive problems, exhaustion."*

Dr. Sharon Goldberg*: "We have evidence of DNA damage, cardiomyopathy, which is the precursor to congestive heart failure."*

"Short- and long-term memory loss. Decreased attention spans. Slower reaction time, even involuntary reactions of muscles, causing the misalignment of spines and jaws."

Dafna Tachover: *"Breast cancer. We find breast cancer in women who have no DNA previous disposition. Disruptive immune function, change in stress protein, reproductive and fertility effects. There are dozens and dozens of studies that show beyond any doubt what this radiation is doing to our sperm. Now if you just take the cell phone out of your pocket the sperm will recuperate within 3 to 4 months. What will not recuperate is the damage to the DNA of the sperm. That is irreparable. The wife of the ex-governor of Indiana was diagnosed with neuroblastoma. Same kind of tumor that Ted Kennedy had, and John McCain had. This is a cell phone brain tumor. LeBron James, one of our sports people, had a salivary gland tumor, another form of cell phone tumor."*

Blake Levitt: *"We are seeing an increase in brain tumors, we are seeing an increase in Alzheimer's, we are seeing increases in all of the neuro-transmitted diseases, ALS, Lou Gehrig's disease, Parkinson's. These are all disease systems that are known to be associated with low level energy exposures.*

Olle Johansson, PhD, Depart. Of Neuroscience Karolinska Institute, Sweden: *"We are talking about 24/7 around the clock exposure. Wherever you are, you will never get away from it. And it seems, from our studies, that maybe your immune system can cope with it for a time; but it will deteriorate, and then the radiation will definitely damage cells that the people have, and the question is, when will that happen?"*

"These are not encouraging papers, so these are not just hypochondriacs thinking there is a problem with this."

56

Dr. Sharon Goldberg: *"This is no longer a subject up for debate when you look at the literature. These effects are seen in all lifeforms, plants, animals, insects, microbes. 5G is not a conversation about whether or not these biological effects exist. They clearly do."*

Barrie Trower, Royal Navy microwave weapons expert: *"I think anyone who puts Wi-Fi into a school, should be locked up for the rest of their life. I really do. I think they are not fit to walk on this earth, because they have not looked at the research and whatever incentive they have, it is not worth the genetic problems that parents are going to have to face with their children as they move forward."*

"France has banned Wi-Fi in their nursery schools. And has put warnings out for regular schools, because they are finding impaired learning capacity in their children when they are around Wi-Fi. They have to put up warning signs where they put up Wi-Fi transmitters."

Dafna Tachover: *"When I got sick and I learned that they were putting Wi-Fi in the schools in Israel, I was very sick at the time, but I could not tolerate the thought that the children in the schools would become as sick as I was. After a few months of correspondence, I submitted a letter to ban the use of Wi-Fi in the schools and replace them with wired networks. The 4 top diseases that are killing our children and young adults right now are brain tumors, thyroid cancer, rectal cancer, and testis cancer. Everywhere where we put our cell phones. A lot of our children are sick, and they are being misdiagnosed and mistreated because a lot of industry has put billions and billions of dollars in the past 30 years to mislead the public as to the health effects and keep the public uninformed."*

Well, there you go again. Keeping us in the dark, controlling the narrative of what's really going on with your true agenda on these issues, including the harmful effects of 5G installation around the world. But back to The Corona Investigative Committee interview with Todd Callender. If you recall in that last video segment, he also shared how this 5G installation occurred at the same time Covid first appeared in Wuhan, China and how the people there were dropping like flies on the street.

Now, is that true? Did that really happen? Well, as you can see here in this article posing the question back on April 26, 2020, Covid first appeared in Wuhan China and how the people there were dropping like flies on the street.
"Did the 5G rollout in Wuhan damage the innate cellular defense cells of the population, putting the people at risk of complications and death from coronavirus?"

Did the 5G rollout in Wuhan damage the innate cellular defense cells of the population, putting the people at risk of complications and death from coronavirus?

And it goes on to say in that article, *"China has completely ignored all warnings and has proceeded to unleash 5G faster than any other nation."*

"In fact, China rolled out 5G in the province of Wuhan in October 2019. Just two months later, the city became afflicted by a new kind of coronavirus named Covid-19."

And they posed the obvious question, "How did a formerly benign class of virus become so opportunistic in such a short amount of time? Why is the death rate so high at the epicenter of the outbreak?"

"Did the 5G launch in Wuhan, China cause widespread compromised immune systems? Why did the city's population suddenly become so vulnerable? Could it be that 5G caused severe inflammation, damaging the immune system?"

And did people really die and drop dead on the streets during this time? Well, check it out for yourself. There were still a few videos left from Wuhan, China that didn't get scrubbed.

This video opens with a person walking down the street in a normal fashion. He comes to a dead stop and falls face down on the concrete. A couple of people come running out of a shop to see if they can assist this person. He doesn't move so they drag him off. Another person in a crowd falls over and doesn't move. A person waiting for a bus just collapses on the street. Another person collapses and an ambulance is called to come pick him up. People collapse as infection spreads throughout Wuhan and surrounding cities. The ambulances are called, but there is nothing that can be done. They are all dead.

Wow! As you can see, as wild as it sounded at first, once you put it all together, it really does appear to be true. There, *"Was an electromagnetic component built in to the Covid Plandemic?"* And *"This involved the installation of 5G technology that was installed around the world at the exact same time Covid-19 was being released upon the world."* And *"The installation of 5G was being done as well in schools across the U.S. and Wuhan, China with people dropping dead in the street."* Which means, it also appeared to be true that, *"It's a dangerous technology with a dual purpose. You can use it to communicate or use it to kill."*

Chapter Four

The Design of Human 2.0

Now, as wild and sickening as that is, that's not the only "deadly consequences" that the Global Elites have in mind, with the installation of this 5G technology, around the world, as well as the Covid Plandemic. Believe it or not, there seems to be another "electromagnetic component" with the 5G technology, specifically on those who took the Covid shots. Could it be that the 5G signal could also be used to trigger a "deadly response" in those who got the shot? Well, let's listen in, as crazy as that sounds, to this next segment of The Corona Investigative Committee Interview.

Todd Callender: *"It so happens that a lot of the tests that we looked at, in the scientific world, focused on the 18 GHz signal and this interplays with the lipid nanoparticle. If you look at the patents of Moderna or Pfizer, the Covid pathogen itself was part bacterial and part viral. We know that now. The pathogens inside the lipid nanoparticle, the ones that were created and are inside the lipid nanoparticles, inside the vaccine, inside the people right now, in some cases are Marburg mixed with E coli. They are Ebola mixed with staphylococcus.*

When those lipid nanoparticles are exposed to an 18 GHz signal they swell and become porous. Which means they will literally pour out those illegal nucleotides, the proteins that will cause these people's bodies to produce these pathogens. That was the whole point of the messenger mRNA technology. It was to genetically modify people for the purpose of having them produce synthetic proteins. In the case of Covid it was synthetic S proteins. After the 18GHz signal it will be other proteins, perhaps M proteins. They also produce, of course, the same HIV protein.

So, when people who are subject to these shots are producing these synthetic proteins, these synthetic pathogens, they are actually shedding them on others. The vaccines were designed to be contagious in the words of Bill Gates. When we look at what is the next shoe to drop, I can already tell you it is Marburg. How do I know that? Because the Marburg Provision of the U.S. Prep Act had already been put into action. Theoretically, there is no Marburg in the United States and hasn't been Marburg in the United States for some time.

How is it that in March of 2020, the Marburg Provisions of the Prep Act were invoked which created funding from centers of Medicaid and Medicare Services, in order to fund the goals of 42CFR part 70 and 71, that's the enabling statute for emergency public health for Health and Human Services. As a part of that, in 2016 you will find that there is a mandate in the public health emergency to quarantine people and test people. They basically have carte blanche, Marshall Law. All constitutional rights are suspended and what rights you get are granted by the CDC. So, when you look at the confluence of all these things, right now, it's up to the Federal Government to cleanse the building with what we call FEMA camps. Quarantine centers. We actually stopped one in Cochise, Arizona. So, it is our contention that these 18 GHz signals will be sent out at some point. It will produce the Marburg Hemorrhagic Fever results, and they will use that as the pretext to fulfill and occupy these quarantine centers."

Okay, now stop right there. It just gets worse as you go! First, we saw the covid vaccine was made with HIV proteins, but now it also contains a concoction of Marburg virus mixed with E coli, and Ebola mixed with staphylococcus. You know, it's like they're trying to get us sick or something! But let's put this to the test. Let's be those Bereans. Are they really mixing viruses in these vaccines to make them even more transmissible?

Stew Peters: *"Karen Kingston is back with us again, and she said she has discovered something in common between all these mysterious, novel, dangerous, deadly viruses that have cropped up and terrified the world for the past few decades. The Marburg virus, the new one with hemorrhagic fever. It's going to spread and break out at the Olympics. HIV, SARS Code 1, SARS Code 2. She says that this common feature is incredible. It's something we can actually use to beat the chaos in conformity that they are imposing on the whole planet so that we don't blow our minds. But what is it? We will have to actually ask. So, what is this commonality that is going to blow our minds.*

Karen Kingston: *"Well one of the commonalities is that we know that these viruses are primarily made in labs, and they have been weaponized. But if you take a look at the common thread, why are they taking the common virus, code-2 of SARS, to an HIV and put it on the back load of Coronavirus, a common cold? Why are they using the flu virus and trying to combine it with things like Ebola and Marburg, or a coronavirus? The answer is because they wanted it to get very transmissible.*

There you have it. They're really doing it and have been for quite some time. They are mixing and matching these viruses to make them more transmissible. Why would you do that? Well, that's why many people are calling this unbelievable behavior for what it is. These Global Elites are creating "bioweapons" that are being used on us and spread around the world for their nefarious purposes! I know it sounds crazy, but as you can see this is really what's going on! Talk about evil!

Let's look at even more proof that not only are these viruses themselves, but even the shots themselves that are being given to people, which are supposed to cure the viruses, but actually don't, are actually spreading the viruses even more! Or as Todd Callender puts it, *"The mRNA technology in the vaccines is causing people to produce a*

62

biological response, that is, create synthetic proteins that then shed or spread to other people. They are designed to be contagious."

Let's first demonstrate, again, that these vaccines are not "safe and effective," and they don't cure people, but rather, frankly, much of the time, they actually kill people.

Dr. Charles Hoffe: *"It makes absolutely no medical sense. Because the fact that they just keep going on with this mantra, that they are safe and effective. Anybody with half a brain should be able to see that they are not safe, and they are not effective. And that the medical authorities are not being honest with the way they keep blaming the failure of this vaccine on the unvaccinated. It's absurd. I think many people are starting to realize that this whole pandemic isn't about a virus, and it isn't about a vaccine, it's about freedom.*

This crop of vaccines has literally the worst safety record of any vaccine in history. I don't know if you have seen the latest numbers from VAERS. Canada doesn't have a vaccine injury reporting system. They pretend to, but I can tell you that I have tried reporting vaccine injuries on my patients fourteen times. And in every case the reports get sent back with the response that these aren't vaccine injuries; they are all coincidences. So, for a doctor in Canada, it seems to be impossible to report a vaccine injury because it gets censored higher up. But in the States, they are not, and they have something called the VAERS. You can look up the numbers.

The latest numbers from two weeks ago showed that they had 18,000 people who are dead from this vaccine. 80 percent of those died within 5 days, 50 percent died within 2 days. 18.000 people dead and 900,000 seriously injured. These are the most dangerous vaccines in history. And calling them vaccine, and I only do that because that is what the media calls them, but they are not vaccines. Vaccines are supposed to be something that makes you immune to the disease. And these do not make you immune to Covid. The hospitals are filled with vaxxed people who are still dying of Covid.

Of course, if they have only had one vax and not quite two weeks after their second vax, they are called unvaccinated in order to try to indict the unvaccinated, to try and blame this on the unvaccinated. But the fact that the authorities are now doing the third shot, it's simple evidence that this shot doesn't work. Two shots never worked so they are trying number 3. In Israel they are on number 4. And it might interest you to know that in Israel a million people never showed up for their third shot. These are neither safe nor effective."

Interviewee: *"By the way, I have Social Security stuff. I have a whole bunch of stuff."*

VigilantFox Reports: *"What kind of stuff?"*

Interviewee: *"Social Security Administration which will give you access to death records and things like that, right?"*

VigilantFox Reports: *"And what does that say?"*

Interviewee: *"We are working through some of that. I haven't made it public yet, and I don't want to yet for a number of reasons. But it's saying that it's a nightmare. It's an absolute nightmare. They are covering up things right and left. Deaths, injuries, the whole nine yards. I mean the vaccines are not vaccines. They are bioweapons. These things are poison. They are killing people. They are damaging people. These are the worst things I have ever seen and the fact that we are forcing people to do it, pushing people to do it, is sick. Every time I see a billboard, that's our tax money trying to convince people to kill their families. It's sick. So, I can't wait to put these guys in jail. I cannot wait. They so deserve it."*

VigilantFox Reports: *"Why do you say that?"*

Interviewee: *"Well, you are killing families. You're injuring people. You know what's going on, and you know that it's dangerous. This is like me trying to market a chainsaw to a two-year-old. Give your toddler a chainsaw. Let him play with it. It's worse than that actually. You don't* *even know what it's doing. Everybody would know that's a stupid idea. You don't know that this is going to kill your kid."*

But they know, and they're still doing it. This is just one of the reasons why we're publishing this, to get this sick, evil, murderous, genocidal behavior, out to the public as fast as we can.

But that's still not all. These Global Elites have also designed these shots for other various evil agendas. Not only to decimate the population, as you've seen, but to also use these so-called vaccines in people to "spread" or "shed" these viruses onto other people. Now, as crazy as that sounds, let's look at that proof.

"COVID-19 vaccine spike proteins are SHEDDING, giving people heart attacks, strokes and more."

NEWSTARGET

UNCENSORED AND INDEPENDENT MEDIA NEWS

HOME   HEALTH FREEDOM   SECOND AMENDMENT   PREPPING   SURVIVAL   CENSORSHIP   SUBSCRIBE   SHOP

COVID-19 vaccine spike proteins are SHEDDING, giving people heart attacks, strokes and more

01/18/2022 / By Arsenio Toledo / Comments

Bypass censorship by sharing this link:

Quote, *"The spike proteins injected into people with the Wuhan coronavirus (COVID-19) vaccine can be shed. The shedding can severely affect the people around the vaccinated person and cause severe health complications such as a heart attack."*

"When people take the mRNA vaccines, the mRNA enters the body and tells it to create what is called the spike protein. This is supposed to help

the body's immune system to detect the COVID-19 virus and get rid of it as soon as it enters the body."

"In reality, the spike proteins being injected into people are at least partially responsible for many of the adverse effects vaccinated people experience. Such as the people being injured or KILLED by the Covid vaccine, because the spike proteins devastate heart cells."

"To make matters worse, the unvaccinated are not safe just because they don't let the dangerous mRNA spike proteins enter their systems."

"For the vaccinated, contact with the spike protein forces the body to make more of it forever. This is what causes many of the health complications associated with it. But when the body makes too much, it can even shed spike proteins."

"This means otherwise healthy unvaccinated people around vaccinated individuals can get the spike proteins in their system. Essentially, all of these vaccinated people are like a bioweapon that has an impact on everyone."

And apparently that impact not only includes "health complications" for the unvaccinated, but even "death" as these reports share.

Stew Peters: *"If you watch fake news on TV, they will tell you that the Covid-19 vaccines are 100 percent safe and anything suggesting otherwise is misinformation. But if you go online, and try to find the information yourself, half the time it will be blocked. They can't have you deciding for yourself. They might get away with all of this, but there's a problem. They can disappear a YouTube video, they can delete Facebook posts, they can ban entire Twitter accounts, but they can't get rid of real people. They can't get rid of a tidal wave of individuals, many of them Joe Biden voters, former backseat supporters who are now telling the world about what has happened to them after getting injected with this Bioweapon being falsely presented as a vaccine.*

One of those people sharing their story with the world is Sarah Stedman. She is a mom that just sent us a letter that I want to read a part of.

Sarah writes, 'My daughter, Ava, age 12, has Celiac Disease, an autoimmune disease. She started her first monthly cycle, her period, in November of 2020 and had no problems until May of 2021. After begging her father, my ex, not to get vaccinated until after we knew more, he decided to get vaccinated anyway. On May 12th, Ava's dad and his wife got the first Pfizer vaccine. On May 16th Ava started bleeding. Everything seemed normal at the time. But on May 21st Ava started feeling anxiety and had a fast heartrate. So, I took her to the emergency room. They did an EKG, but no lab work. The doctor refused because he doesn't do lab work for just anxiety. (Okay doc, I got it.) On May 29th, I took her to UC San Diego urgent care and asked for lab work. He said the fingerprint and hemoglobin was 5.9, which is critically unstable.

I was told to get Ava to Children Hospital, she was admitted, given 2 units of blood, placed on birth control and iron pills, and sent home. On June 2nd, Ava's dad and his wife got the second Pfizer vaccine. (Very noble, upstanding) On June 11th, Ava had lab work directly from her left arm and produced jelly-like clotting blood that was very abnormal. On June 23rd during an appointment at UC San Diego, the doctor assured us that sometimes, abnormal bleeding can happen, but she had never seen it in a pediatric patient.'

So, the letter goes on like this for a while in a steady pattern, with her daughter having this abnormally heavy bleeding and birth control pills weren't controlling it. Eventually Sarah took her daughter to a doctor of Holistic Medicine Specialists, who says the bleeding is caused by transmission of the Bioweapon through vaccine shedding. The specialist claimed that she had seen many such cases in the past year. So, your daughter who has not been inoculated is ill due to being in close proximity to her father and his wife who are vaccinated. And this is what a medical professional has told you."

Breaking News: *"It's not just cell towers that give people heart attacks these days, it's the vaccines as well. The reason why the vaccines are giving people heart attacks is because of the spike protein that's in the vaccine. But the vaccines don't just contain spike protein, they force your body to make spike protein, forever. And that's a problem. Because all the vaccinated people out there are eventually going to have heart attacks, just like these athletes on television. Or they are going to get strokes. Or they are going to get other issues. Pilots are dropping out of the sky like never before. Just research small plane crashes.*

The vaccinated are like a new disease. But what makes matters worse is that the vaccinated are making so many spike proteins that it's outgassing, shedding into the environment around them. Otherwise, healthy unvaccinated people are going to get strokes with this spike protein. The television keeps telling us about Covid and the like, but the real story is the spike. Everybody knows it was the worst idea possible to encode the spike protein in mRNA and inject it into people. Gene therapy, the mass-produced spike protein, it's a nightmare. But essentially, all these vaccinated people are like a bioweapon, giving those around them heart attacks and strokes."

And a whole host of other problems because they now shed it on to you! And if that wasn't sick and bad enough, these same Global Elites are not only using this same Bioweapon technology to create spike protein factories inside of people to "spread" or "shed" these viruses to even more of the population, as you just saw, but they are also even planning on using their so-called "vaccines" to "spread" or "shed to others" who didn't want them in the first place, guaranteeing that everyone is going to get their shots whether they wanted them or not. Here's just some of that proof!

"Moderna Wants to Transform the Body into a Vaccine-Making Machine."

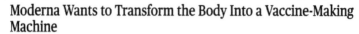

Moderna Wants to Transform the Body Into a Vaccine-Making Machine

The U.S. company and its German rival BioNTech plan to use RNA as a messenger inside cells to produce an immune reaction. The advance could upend vaccine development long after the pandemic.

By Robert Langreth and Naomi Kresge

Almost every antiviral vaccine ever sold works in a similar way: A dead or weakened virus, or a piece of one, is introduced into a healthy person. The weakened virus stimulates the immune system to generate antibodies, protecting the person when the real pathogen threatens to infect them.

Over the decades, this tried-and-true approach has vanquished polio, eradicated smallpox, and reined in chicken pox, measles, and mumps. But vaccine production has never been simple or fast. Many flu vaccines are still grown in chicken eggs. Newer approaches draw on genetic engineering to eliminate the need for whole viruses, but their viral proteins are still grown inside live cells.

The coronavirus vaccines from Moderna Inc., in Cambridge, Mass., and its German rival BioNTech SE propose to immunize people in a radically different way: by harnessing human cells to become miniature vaccine factories in their own right. Instead of virus proteins, the vaccines contain genetic instructions that prompt the body to produce them.

"Vaccines of the future could be as contagious as viruses."

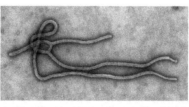

And notice it was 2017, which shows us they've been working on this for quite some time. And here's a recent development showing how they pulled it off. **"Scientists Developing Controversial 'Contagious Vaccines' Designed as "Recombinant Viruses" That Spread from Vaccinated to Unvaccinated."**

Scientists Developing Controversial 'Contagious Vaccines' Designed as "Recombinant Viruses" That Spread From Vaccinated to Unvaccinated

Each of these new vaccines are so called recombinant viruses

Scientists are currently developing "self-spreading vaccines" aimed at infecting others from vaccinated to unvaccinated populations, according to National

"Scientists are currently developing 'self-spreading vaccines' aimed at infecting others from vaccinated to unvaccinated populations, according to National Geographic."

"The vaccine would essentially infect anybody within a close enough proximity to the inoculated individual, so that one person could potentially spread the vaccine to many other unsuspecting people."

"Imagine a cure that's as contagious as the disease it fights – a vaccine that could replicate in a host's body and spread to others nearby, quickly and easily protecting a whole population from the next pandemic."

"That's the goal of several teams around the world who are reviving controversial research to develop self-spreading vaccines."

"But because of the 'extremely high-risk and international nature of this work' and the 'irreversible' consequences, this experimental research faces numerous ethical and legal hurdles."

No kidding! But they're still doing it anyway, as these people share.

The David Knight Show: *"They say that shedding is simply a conspiracy theory, they are bragging about how they are going to make a contagious vaccine that will essentially shed and spread."*

Narrator: *"Since the outbreak of Covid-19, the virus has been leading the major headlines as well as our daily lives. Did you know that one approach to control these diseases is by releasing a virally transmitted vaccine? Unlike traditional vaccines, infectious vaccines do not require*

any individual consent. Solutions are also being developed with food and agriculture, and they are currently making their way to the regulatory approval process."

The David Knight Show: *"Mandates may no longer matter as scientists create contagious vaccines that spread by themselves. Force may no longer be needed to achieve a 100 percent vaccination rate. A new and extremely controversial vaccination technology is being tested to stop the spread of various diseases. And it is an authoritarian, mad scientist's dream."*

And I would agree, but it's obviously going to lead to some pretty nightmarish, irreversible results. Did you catch that one part where they were also looking at spreading these vaccines into people "against their own consent" not just with the vaccines, but even using this "infectious model" in the food supply? Surely, they're not looking at doing that as well, are they? Well, unfortunately they are. Here's just two examples, one from the U.S. and the other from the U.K.

"Researchers aim to develop edible plant-based mRNA vaccines."

"The future of vaccines may look more like eating a salad than getting a shot in the arm. University of California Riverside scientists are studying whether they can turn edible plants like lettuce into mRNA vaccine factories."

And across the pond they admit it with this blunt statement. **"Scientists are developing plants that can deliver same vaccine technology used by Pfizer and Moderna Covid shots by being EATEN."**

"When a person thinks of vaccines, they often imagine the long needle of a syringe before a slight pinch on their arm, followed by a day of soreness as they recover."

"That could soon change as researchers attempt to deliver messenger RNA (mRNA) vaccine technology via edible plants."

"They are hoping that they can grow vegetables that can deliver vaccines with the same technology used to develop the Pfizer-BioNTech and Moderna COVID-19 vaccines."

"The plants could have a huge impact on peoples' lives."

Yeah, the understatement of the year there. And that plan is to do this with a bunch of different kinds of foods we eat. Watch this.

Narrator: *"As billionaires and Big Tech increasingly take over agriculture and the food we eat, we ask, 'Are we being turned into a genetically modified food colony?' Could plant based vaccines save the* *world? Scientists say, 'Rice, corn, potatoes or lettuce could be used to produce antibodies.'"*

Yuri Kleba, Molecular Biologist: *"It's a kind of complex process which starts by the procedure that infects them with foreign DNA, genetic material, which reprograms them to stop doing everything else and just make one protein which is the medicine that you want to produce."*

Narrator: *"Biotech farms are already in clinical trials with their plant-based drugs, are waiting for approval from Health Agencies to combat Ebola and Covid-19."*

Ben Fajzullin, DW News Reports: *"This isn't just about pleasing vegans. A plant based Covid jab would be cheaper and quicker. Instead of using hamster ovaries or monkey kidneys, you can use veggies or even tobacco."*

In other words, pretty much anything in the food supply. So, I get it now. No wonder these same Global Elites have also been buying up all the farmland and controlling our food supply. Apparently, they're making sure there's no way of escaping from their Genetic Manipulation. You're going to get your genetically modified shots into your bodies one way or another, whether you wanted it or not. How sick is this? Unfortunately, it gets even sicker. Let's now move on to the next statement made by Todd Callender in The Corona Investigative Committee Interview.

"Is the Marburg Virus really what these Global Elites are planning on producing next with those who got the vaccine using an "electronic signal" and were these advanced plans outlined with something called The Marburg Provisions Prep Act?"

Now, notice in that last video how they said this is just one of the justifications for genetically modifying our food supply and forcing us into getting their vaccines into us, one way or another. It was to supposedly help against Ebola, Covid, or Marburg. What's up with that? I mean, last time I checked, currently there's no Marburg or Ebola outbreak around the planet. The key word there is "currently." You see, maybe that's all about to change with a "trigger" these Elites have designed inside our bodies, at least those bodies of those who got the shots. And that this "triggering" is a viral response with an "electronic signal."

Could it be, as Todd Callender said, that these Global Elites are laying the groundwork for yet another way to spread or shed or create these viruses inside of people against their own will, using an "electronic signal?" I mean, if they can't get you to volunteer for the shot, they'll just "shed" the virus or vaccine on you through other people, or even the food supply. Or just in case somehow you escape that procedure, they'll produce it in those who got the shots with an "electronic signal" and then off onto you. Is that true? I mean, that's the stuff of fantasy, right? Unfortunately, no, not anymore!

Chapter Five

The Control of Human 2.0

Believe it or not, it's another horrific nightmare these wicked Global Elites have dreamed up for us with, wait for it, the 5G electronic signal. You see, doctors are starting to blow the whistle on just what else was contained within those vaccines, which are not vaccines, and what else these new ingredients will allow them to do inside people's bodies by emitting the right "electronic signal." Let's listen in to just one doctor exposing the whole plan.

Dr. Carrie Madej: *"You can read this stuff online. Many organizations say that 2030 is when we become part Cyborg. All of us, without our consent. They don't need our consent, supposedly. And they mean that literally. So, how do you become part Cyborg? Well, first of all, they can get us to be linked in with 'the internet of everything.' Literally you would be a walking computer bit. You'd walk around and interact with any smart device anywhere. When that happens, it's a two-way communication. So, you're putting out information, or maybe you're giving commands to your printer or your stove or whatever. Maybe that's okay. You're also getting input into your body as well.*

So, you could get commands into your body, and you wouldn't even know what commands were yours, or what's coming from outside of you. They were proposing to do this in this city, Atlanta, Georgia, last year but they were behind their timeline. What they want to do is get something of a biosensor inside of your body, which is like a computer bit; they are microscopic. They can be inhaled, but they found they weren't very efficient through inhalation to get the payload in. So, they decided injection or microneedle patches were the best way to get the payload to a high enough level so that when it's turned on, you are automatically connected to everything.

So, that's one way that's going to be the social credit system. That's how you get your cryptocurrency, the digital ID. So, you're just a product in the store. That's a way to control society very quickly, because you would be considered a good human or bad human depending on what you thought. Even predictive policing is involved. So, Bill Gates actually has his own little advertisement for West Africa and because they're doing this biometric surveillance on the people there, right now. In his own description, he says, 'Well, once we have it perfected here in West Africa, it's coming to all the developed countries.

So, there in Africa, their vaccine, whether or not they got the vaccine, will allow them to have services or money or necessities. Also, all their information is in there. So, it's all going to be inside your body. You'll be the walking computer bit. That's one thing. But the biosensors have a bigger description called hydrogel. Hydrogel is the main kind of word used for all of these things that these nanobots can do. They are microscopic, they put millions of them in one syringe needle. They can replicate and grow on their own. They actually can grow more inside your body. It sounds unbelievable but they can do it.

They can assemble and disassemble and reassemble into innumerable things and they can do some good things. They can repair a tendon if you tore it, they can be looking for a tumor cell and attack it right away. Those are the good things. But they have also been looking into things, you know, Elon Musk and the Defense Advanced Research Projects Agency; they are looking at different things than that. They are very interested in our brains, and they know that hydrogel has an affinity for our nervous system. So, the nerves and the brain tissue, the hydrogel will go there. Well, when there is enough of it there, you can actually download other people's memories, similar to the matrix, where you're downloading languages or how to do karate. So, that might sound nice, because you don't go to school anymore. You just download everything. But, who's in control of that?

It's a computer that's in control of that. I mean that's frightening. Different things can be downloaded. You would lose your sense of reality. Also know that they can, by N3 technology, and Elon Musk has something to do with this as well, they can rewrite a memory in your brain. Meaning, you would not know what memory was yours or not. An event could be rewritten. The history of your life could be rewritten.

There is something called 'The Clarity Project' that people should look up, because that's when the hydrogel is actually melding with the brain tissue where, if someone gets into the computer program, they can see everything you see through your eyes. They have been successful using this with this kind of technology with pilots for 15 plus years in the military with their different aircraft; where the pilots wear the helmet, they get injected with the substance, and then the pilot just thinks it, and the aircraft does it. They move their eyes, and the aircraft does it. They become one with the machine. Literally, one with the machine.

This sounds Sci-Fi. It sounds like, 'Oh my gosh, this is never going to happen,' but you have to listen to the people pushing the agenda. You have to know what they are telling us. If you listen to Boris Johnson, he's saying the same thing. He's saying that you will walk around, and no thought will ever be your thought alone. Every thought will always be known, all the time, nothing is hidden. He even said your Alexa will be giving you commands, and you won't even know it's Alexa giving you commands. You'll think it's your thoughts.

Listen to these crazy people. They will tell you what they want to do. They think that 2030 is the goal. So, that would be loss of autonomy, privacy, and constant surveillance. Also, this mishmash of what is your reality and what is not. This is the turning over from Human 1.0 to Human 2.0, becoming less organic, becoming more into the cyborg. They can actually, literally, start it from the inside out. This is their idea. Doesn't mean they are going to get away with it. So that's the endpoint, and I also go into the genetics of that, because, in these scientific meetings I attend, they talked about how they're very interested in patenting the genetic genes genome. They tried to patent human genes that were natural to us, and they got turned down. Thank goodness. Because no one should own anything, a tree, or a vitamin, but they were able to successfully patent anything synthetic.

The Supreme Court in the United States ruled that even a human can be owned if anything synthetic is inside of you. So, why I'm on the alarm call to the world is that these particular vaccines, which are really gene modification injections, have the potential, they are synthetic, if any of their genetic material gets taken up into our genome, and there are ways that they can do it, overnight, technically, you would be owned, part or all of you, by the Department of Defense, The Gates Foundation, any one of these scientists, military, who knows who, whoever owns that patent. This is unbelievable, unconscionable, that this is even going on, and this needs to stop."

Again, the understatement of the year. But let's unpack this. There's so much going on in this interview with this doctor. Is what she said true? Did they really, "Put something else inside these vaccines that electronically connects us to a global matrix system that will act as a "biosensor" that will continually monitor our health and continually track us and continually give our bodies instructions?" Is that true? Yes! "Biosensors" are what they're called, and they have been worked on for quite some time now. In fact, here's DARPA, once again, the Defense Advanced Research Project Agency, admitting it way back in 2018.

60 Minutes Reports: *"It might surprise you to learn that many of the innovations deployed to counter the Coronavirus were once obscured Pentagon funded projects to defend soldiers from contagious diseases and biological weapons. The lifesaving vaccine that was developed in record* *time owes a debt to these programs. To learn more, we met the man who has been leading the rapid vaccine effort, Retired Colonel Matt Hepburn, an army infectious disease physician. He spent years with the secretive Defense Advanced Research Projects Agency, or DARPA, working on technology he hopes will ensure Covid-19 is the last pandemic."*

Dr. Matt Hepburn: *"If we want to say we can never let this happen again, we are going to have to go even faster."*

60 Minutes Reports: *"Eight years ago Dr. Hepburn was recruited by DARPA."*

Dr. Matt Hepburn: *"The DARPA director was very clear. 'Your mission is to take pandemics off the table.'"*

60 Minutes Reports: *"Sounds impossible."*

Dr. Matt Hepburn: *"Of course. And that was the beauty of the DARPA model. We challenge the research community to come up with solutions that may sound like Science Fiction and were very willing to take chances with high-risk investments that may not work. But if they do, we can completely transform the landscape."*

President Eisenhower: *"Good Morning, Ladies and Gentlemen."*

60 Minutes Reports: *"More than 60 years ago, DARPA was born after President Eisenhower was caught off guard when Russia launched the first satellite, Sputnik, into orbit."*

Reporter asking Pres. Eisenhower a question: *"I ask you sir, what are we going to do about it?"*

60 Minutes Reports: *"The small Defense Department Agency was given a single purpose. Prevent surprises like that from ever happening again. So, Dr. Hepburn finds academics, companies, inventors working in their garages and pushes them to deliver."*

Dr. Hepburn: *"What we don't do, we don't say okay, here's our problem. Here's your blank check. Come back to us in three to five years, and we'll see how you're doing."*

60 Minutes Reports: *"You're on them?"*

Dr. Hepburn: *"Active program management is what we call it, okay."*

60 Minutes Reports: *"Dr. Hepburn showed us a few current projects. Some sound like they are from an episode of Star Trek. Consider a ship like the USS Theodore Roosevelt, hobbled last year when 1271 crew members tested positive for the Coronavirus. What if everyone on board had their health monitored with a subdermal implant. Now in late-stage testing, Its not some dreaded government microchip to track your every move, but a tissue like gel engineered to continuously test your blood."*

Dr. Hepburn: *"It's a sensor. The tiny green thing in there, you put it underneath your skin and what that tells you is that there are chemical reactions going on inside the body, and that signal means you are going to have symptoms tomorrow."*

60 Minutes Reports: *"There's an actual transmitter in that?"*

Dr. Hepburn: *"Yes, it's like a check engine light."*

60 Minutes Reports: *"Check this sailor out before he infects other people."*

Dr. Hepburn: *"That's right."*

60 Minutes Reports: *Sailors would get the signal and then self-administer a blood draw and test themselves on site."*

Dr. Hepburn: *"We can have that information in 3-5 minutes. As you diagnose and treat, what you do is stop the infection in its tracks."*

Col. Matt Hepburn, MD, USA, Biological Technologies Office, DARPA: *"I am an active-duty Army infectious disease physician and have specialized in addressing biological threats that can either be engineered or naturally occurring, such as Ebola or pandemic influenza. Today we are going to be talking about one of the technologies that I actively manage, a company called Profusa, which is aiming at achieving tissue-level continuous health monitoring. Through the SBIR program, we funded them to solve an incredible technical challenge that no one had previously been able to solve.*

The key innovation that was presented to us, as they said, 'Why can't we make a chemical substance that's really identical to what's underneath the skin, called the subcutaneous tissue, so that your body doesn't recognize it as a foreign body response.' It incorporates itself into the tissue. We have a lot of examples now where the sensor is put right under the skin and will sense things like oxygen and other chemicals that are very important to our metabolism. And that's not just to sense for a day or a week or a month, but we imagine that sensing these parameters could go on for a period of years.

One of the most important applications to us is so that we can improve the health of our worldwide deployed military forces. We feel a strong sense of obligation that if we are going to ask somebody to be deployed to carry out their mission, we need to keep them healthy. This technology will give us a way to monitor if someone is getting sick. We imagine that we could sense that very early and therefore prevent them from getting sick and prevent complications, allowing them to stay healthy and continue to carry out their mission. In addition, if our technology translates into general health benefits, we are very excited about that. So, in other words we fund those national security applications. The company finds private sector partnership funding for that general health benefit, and we see it as really a win-win as this technology develops."

In other words, it's not just for the military. It's for all of us. But notice, these "biosensors" will continuously monitor a person's bodily functions and status and "tell" if you're getting sick so they can "prevent" it from happening? Well, how are they going to do that? Are they going to send out an "electronic signal" and genetically modify us for our own good, whether we wanted it or not?

Well, let's go back to the "biosensor" that allows them to do this inside of us. Apparently, the first step in achieving this continual biosensor capability in not just soldiers, but the whole human race, was to get that type of technology platform inside all of us. It's called mRNA and it was inside the Covid shots, as seen here.

MSNBC Reports: *"I am joined now by MSNBC news and global correspondent, Willem Marx. So, what do we know about these two companies partnered up to develop this vaccine?"*

Willem Marx: *"Well, it's really the German company's proprietary biotechnology that has been key to this breakthrough. That technology relies on something called messenger RNA, mRNA, that occurs naturally in all of our bodies. It's essentially a molecule made up with hundreds of building blocks, sometimes hundreds sometimes thousands, called nucleotides, and it works like an instruction manual to our cells. It essentially is introduced to a cell and instructs it how to act. So, what they have done with this particular vaccine, they tweaked the mRNA and made it into an instruction manual to the cells, telling them to create a specific protein, an immunogen. You might have heard of the spike protein in the last few months.*

That's what this does. It encourages the cells to create spike proteins which in turn provoke an immune response in our bodies and that means that antibodies are created so that they can attack the virus if it shows up in our systems. What's so encouraging about this recent data is so many in the vaccine development try to target that spike protein, and the experts say this is really hopeful. I've been speaking to some of the doctors and scientists involved in this Pfizer and BioNTech vaccine, speaking to them about this recently, and when I talked to one of the men about this, Mark Mulligan, he runs the NYU Langone and Vaccine Center, he's the Director, in treating some of his patients, he said that the underlying basis, not just for this vaccine but all future vaccines, what is so incredible about this mRNA technology is that it can be tweaked and built upon as required. Take a listen:"

Mark Mulligan, NYU Langone Vaccine Center Director: *"The revolution will come in that it's a very rapid platform once you have the superstructure, if you will. You can slide in a new gene, whether it's for HIV or something else once you've got the superstructure mRNA."*

Willem Marx: *"So, even the platform that supports this potential vaccine that could hopefully combat this pandemic is so important. It could be a platform that could form the basis of weapons for all future vaccines to fight all future viral pandemics."*

Boy, did we get duped. That is, those who got the Covid vaccine. It's not a vaccine. It's a man-made genetic program, called mRNA, that will then give "program instructions" to your body, not just for Covid-19 supposedly, but what? For all future pandemics! It's a "programmable platform" to genetically modify people for the rest of their lives. He just admitted it! And lest you think these so-called vaccine companies can be trusted, that are creating these vaccines that are really not vaccines, but "programmable platforms" for future genetic manipulation of people, this "biosensing technology" and "programmable platform" that's inside these shots are just the beginning of what they've crammed in there.

Now that other doctors have gotten their hands on some of these so-called vaccines, the ingredients they've discovered in the vials are showing all kinds of strange contents. Watch this.

Dr. Carrie Madej: *"First of all, in July, a local lab in Georgia, they wanted me to examine contents of a vial that they had just received. The vial was fresh. It had already been used to be injected into at least one patient because it was the end of the day, and they were going to discard it. So, they were able to get the vial. This particular vial was Moderna. I was there to witness them getting some of the contents on a glass slide with a compound microscope so I could look at it. Nothing was added to* *the solution, nothing was diluted, no human tissue was added, only the white light from the microscope. Over time it was becoming more room temperature from the refrigeration.*

So, first, it was just translucent. And then as time went on, about 2 hours, colors appeared. I had never seen anything like this. It was like a chemical reaction happening. It was a brilliant blue and royal purple and yellow and sometimes green. So, these appeared, and I didn't know what that was. After further investigating, more super conducting materials can do that with bright light being admitted to it. Super conducting materials would be like an injectable commuting system. These fibers were appearing more and more. Some of the fibers had a little cube structure on them. I'm not sure what that was. Also, there were metallic fragments in there. They were not metallic fragments I was used to seeing. They were more exotic.

At the edge of the cover slide, the glass slip that you put on a glass partition, top of the glass slide, there are edges. So, all these colors started to move to the edge and there was self-assembling going on and they were growing. They were synthetic. There was one particular object or organism, not sure what you would call it, that had tentacles coming from it. It was able to lift itself up off of the cover or the glass slide."

Stew Peters: *"Was it alive? Was this thing alive?"*

Dr. Carrie Madej: *"Yeah. It appeared to be self-aware. It was able to grow or move. All I can tell you is that this is not something they taught us in medical school, nothing in my laboratories, nothing I have seen before. I showed this to other people in the field and they don't know what it is either. When I first saw this and I kept looking over and over again, I had another colleague with me, we both thought it seems like it was self-aware, like it knows we are watching it. It was an intuition, a feeling of mine. It was very upsetting.*

So, after about 2 or 2 ½ hours we destroyed it, of course. So, I thought maybe this was a fluke. Maybe it was just that one vial. So, just recently the lab got more vials in from the same manufacturer but a different batch. Looking at it the same way under my compound microscope, another one of those tentacled life structures appeared completely under the cover slip. There was no movement because it wasn't on the edge. I couldn't believe I saw another one. It was the same thing. Colors appeared over time, fibers, this time, if they do it again, I got a video of them.

There was actually motion in the video. This is very concerning, and I was also able to look at the contents of a Johnson and Johnson vial and there was definitely a substance that looks like graphene, they all had graphene like structures, whether or not they were I don't have the capability of testing them in this lab, but that is what they appeared to be. They had fatty substances, a sticky glue-like substance that would be considered a hydrogel, in both of them, right.

That means they are lying to us. They are lying to us about the J & J not having nano lipid particles or anything of that substance. In the J & J they also had different colors. They had fluorescent, pastel colors. And again, a lot of synthetic structures in there as well. In the J & J, the spherical ring structures. A lot of sphere structures. I'm describing what I see, but I have never seen anything like this before.

These things should not be in these injections or what they are falsely calling vaccines. What are they going to do to somebody? What are they going to do to a child? I started crying when I saw these. The second time when I saw these under the microscope, it was a confirmation of what I saw the first time."

Stew Peters: *"If I were to look under a microscope and I saw something that I was told was a vaccine to promote health and safety and some self-aware tentacle equipped creature started moving, I would probably run out of the laboratory. That's just me. I'm not scared of a lot, but that is scary that that is going into the blood of global citizens, and you're right. They want to push this into our children."*

Gee, it's almost like they're cramming this into the bodies of the whole world as fast as they can. I wonder why? Could it be to have a "programmable platform" into the whole human race, so they can then connect you to a Global Matrix system called 5G that will then continually monitor you and your body continuously, and maybe even genetically manipulate you from afar, as this article shares.

"DARPA Hydrogel in COVID Vaccine can create crystals, nano-antennas to receive signals from 5G Tower."

DARPA Hydrogel in COVID Vaccine can create crystals, nano-antennas to receive signals from 5G Tower

goldenproject.org/documentfiles/Analysis-of-test-sticks-from-surface-testing-in-the-Slovak-Republic.pdf

DARPA Hydrogel & lithium mixture immediately reacts with living structures to form crystals that are directionally oriented to the pineal gland, which has its own electromagnetic field.

The crystals are conductive due to the lithium contained in it. The crystals can receive the signal from the transmitter to the cell and transmit signals from the cell to the transmitter. These are actually nano-antennas.

Figure 10 to 11. After contact of the Darpa Hydrogel with organic fluids (e.g., saliva), within a few minutes they begin to form rectangular crystal structures. There gradually grow in a fractal manner.

And this is why that doctor went on to say, *"There is a battle raging for humanity. Big Tech collaborates with Big Pharma to introduce new technologies in the coming vaccines that will alter our DNA and turn us into hybrids. This will end humanity as we know it and start the process of transhumanism or what they call HUMAN 2.0."*

"The plans are to use vaccines to inject nanotechnology into our bodies and connect us to the Cloud and Artificial Intelligence. This will enable corrupt governments and tech giants to control us, without us being aware of it."

Quote, *"They are actually 'nano-antennas.'"* And lest you doubt that this is what's inside these vaccines, that are not vaccines, this is why Japan pulled some of the vaccines out of circulation that were sent their way.

"Japan discovers "magnetic" substance in Pfizer covid vaccines; journalists start DYING from the vax they pushed."

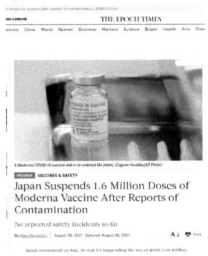

And **"Japan Suspends 1.6 Million Doses of Moderna Vaccine After Reports of Contamination."**

And I quote, *"Foreign materials found in some unused vials of U.S. biotechnology company Moderna's COVID-19 vaccine in Japan may have had pieces of metal, sources at the Japanese health ministry said Thursday."*

"The ministry believes that the foreign objects may have been mixed in with the vaccine vials during the manufacturing process."

In other words, it was done deliberately. Shocker! But you might be thinking, "Well, how come I haven't heard about all this?" Well again, because as we covered in our other documentary, ***Subliminal Seduction: How the Mass Media Mesmerizes the Minds of the Masses,*** they are controlling everything that we see, hear, or read, on anything, certainly the Covid Plandemic. And anybody who tries to get the truth by other means, they are now being killed for doing so. Don't believe me? Here's just one quick example.

Stew Peters: *"Well as you know the Stew Peters show features more whistleblowers than any other platform and we have oftentimes told you* *that being a real whistleblower can be dangerous. Not like the fake Facebook whistleblowers, but real ones. Nurses blowing the whistle on what they are seeing in their hospitals, the murder for money schemes, people blowing the whistle from inside the biotech companies, talking about these bioweapons being falsely referred to as a vaccine. All this can be very dangerous. You can be cancelled, deplatformed, or even outcast from social groups. Deanna Lorraine is here with us right now to tell us how actually dangerous being a real whistleblower can be. Thanks a lot for being here."*

Deanna Lorraine: *"This is a really important message for all whistleblowers out there, nurses, doctors, persons who are out there blowing the whistle. A doctor, Andreas Noack, from Germany, you may have seen his videos, he's been an active whistleblower against the lockdowns, against the vaccines, since Covid first started. What actually happened in November of 2020, he was doing a livestream talking about the dangers of the vaccines and the lockdown and he actually got raided by the German police. He was raided while his livestream was going on. He was raided, arrested, got his home raided, everything.*

Now just last week he released a very important video on graphene oxide being in the vaccine. The video went viral, it was huge. He was talking about how graphene oxide is absolutely in all the vaccines and it's very dangerous that it acts like little knives in your blood stream, cutting your blood vessels, etc. The video blew up. That was on November 23rd, last week. This past weekend, November 27th, his pregnant wife announced in a video that he had been brutally attacked, and he had been killed. I'm not joking. This is just one week later after the release of his viral video about graphene oxide being in the vaccine."

Wow! So much for freedom of the press, let alone free speech. This is really going on folks, and this is why you're not hearing about it in general. These Global Elites are killing the same people who expose what's really going on and what's really inside the contents of these vaccines, which are not really vaccines! In fact, here's another article talking about this particular murder.

"Leading German Chemist Andreas Noack Dies 30 Minutes After Exposing Graphene Oxide, Possibly Assassinated."

No possibilities, it was. And that's from the European Union Times. And for those who have eyes to see and ears to hear, believe it or not, these Global Elites have even admitted this is what they want to do to us, i.e., connect us "electronically" around the globe, so they can monitor us and "adjust" us biologically, if needed, on the fly. Again, they call it Human 2.0. And they were discussing this "upgrade" for all of us, whether we want it or not,

way back in 2019 at the World Economic Forum in Davos, Switzerland. You know, just before Covid hit, as seen here. Watch this.

Joseph Cahill, Senior Vice President, Finance and Administration PMI: *"Today's theme is Humans 2.0, designing and implementing future proof strategy. In a recent Brightline study, 59 percent of senior executives admit that their organizations struggle to bridge the gap between strategy and implementation. It's easy of course to be enamored with new strategies and brand-new technologies. But it is much more important to recognize that all strategic change is implemented through action plans and projects themselves."*

Ricardo Vargas, Executive Director, The Brightline Initiative: *"What we see today is an absolute massive development of technology. We move technology at a lightning speed. Computers are faster. AI, VR, everything is moving faster, but the humans keep moving at the same speed."*

90

Rainer Strack, Senior partner and managing director, Boston Consulting Group: *"When we talk about the future of work, you have to understand really what kind of mega trends are hitting our workforce. Number one is shifts in technology and digital productivity. So, automation, AI, robotics, analytics. Number two, data, access, access to people etc. So, the first three things are all about digital and this is probably the mega trend of mega trends. And finally, people are looking for purpose. So, purpose and well-being."*

Ricardo Vargas: *"You don't work only for money, but you work to accomplish something and bring everybody together."*

Bernadette Wightman, Managing director, resources, manufacturing and logistics, global services, BT Group: *"So, as leaders I think it's really important that we show them. We'll show everyone where we are going, and we take everybody with us as well."*

What kind of gobbly gook, quasi-spiritual, planetary existence are these Elites creating for us? They say with all this technology they're "going to bring everybody together" and they're "bringing everybody with you as well" i.e., whether we want it or not, into this Human 2.0. And as crazy as that sounds folks, this new Human 2.0 that they're building for us clearly involves a new "enhanced" humanity.

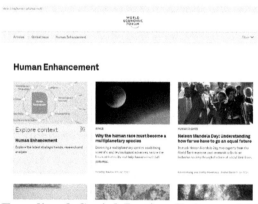

"Information and Transparency, Enhanced Genes, Enhanced Bodies, Equality & Social Justice, Enhanced Minds, Humanness & Autonomy, and Longevity."

Excuse me? Are you going to dictate how long we get to live in your new Human 2.0 world that you're creating? But wait a second. How are you going to give all of us this new enhanced information and so-called social equality and longevity and enhanced genes, bodies, and minds?

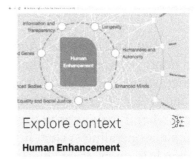

Well, can you say a 5G Global electronic signal that effects some sort of internal genetic programmable platform inside of us, you know, those that got the Covid shot? You see, it just so happens another huge plank of the World Economic Forum's vision for our future, Human 2.0, as seen here is what they call the Strategic Intelligence plan.

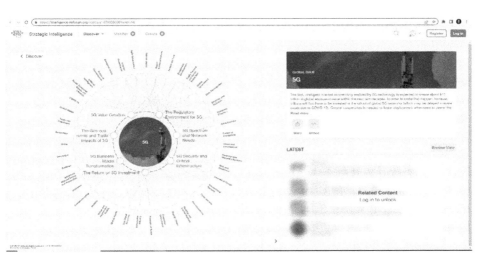

And it says right there on that global map that this Strategic Intelligence plan is going to be used to control such things around the whole planet, such as Covid, Mobility, Global Health, the Digital Economy, Banking & Capital Markets, Financial & Monetary Systems, Supply Chains, Retail Consumer Goods & Lifestyle, Global Governance, and the Internet of Things, just to name a few. Anybody starting to smell a rat here? I think most of us can start to put all the pieces together with what they're sharing about the future they're creating for us, out of their own mouths and websites. Human 2.0. is clearly about total human control.

But wait a second. Again, how are they going to create this new and improved version of humanity they call Human 2.0 across the whole planet, where they will control anything and everything and even monitor us and give us these so-called "enhancements" or "upgrades" on the fly? Well, what if they were to trick us into injecting a programmable computer operating system inside our bodies that acts as an antenna that responds to an external "electronic signal" called 5G, that allows them to continually track and monitor us and give our bodies instructions and enhancements electronically. Sounds crazy, doesn't it? Unfortunately, here's just one of their propaganda videos simplifying it for the rest of us, what this new, Human 2.0, future that they're building for us looks like. Watch this.

Quantified Self Revolution: *"Your trivial seeming self-tracking app is part of something much bigger. It's part of a new stage in the scientific method, another tool in the kit. It's not the only thing going on, but it's part of that evolutionary process."*

Narrator: *"So you hear a lot of talk these days about the 'Quantified Self-Revolution.' Everything is being tracked. We have metrics for everything. We're extending sensors into everything, and all of a sudden creating an influx of data. So, everything is tracked online. Now everything is being tracked in our body. We live in a world in which human beings have been reduced – have been turned into algorithmic cascades of data. And most people are terrified of this notion of infinite tracking.*

But I think the 'Quantified Self-Revolution' potentially can reveal us to ourselves. It can become the ultimate mirror. You know what happens when the algorithm cascades? These observers, human beings, will now be able to see themselves as structures, as patterns amidst the data. We will be able to take data sets of millions of people, measuring millions of metrics of data, to find patterns and find spaces of interconnection or find emergent self-organization that is occurring on these mega-patterns and then, these different scales.

We'll get what Steven Johnson calls the long view. We'll get the equivalent of the microscope or the telescope for units of information for data sets. Who knows what we might learn about ourselves? How might we be able to take that data and use those insights to feed them back into us, right? Creating that effect of moment of ontological design, where that information accesses feedback that further changes how we act and changes how we optimize the world and society. The 'Quantified Self-Revolution' is an upgrade for this operating system, this man-machine operating system. It's Human version 2.0"

Doesn't that sound wonderful? Are you kidding me? They're treating us like some collective Borg in their sick, twisted future. What are we? Just a bunch of…human cattle…to you guys? Yeah, apparently. And did you read that opening statement? *"Your trivial seeming self-tracking app is part of something much bigger. It's part of a new stage in the scientific method, another tool in the kit. It's not the only thing going on, but it's part of that evolutionary process."*

Well, gee, that's comforting! What are you going to do? Turn us into something different? Yes, they call it, bluntly, Human 2.0. The so-called evolutionary upgrade that these Global Elites want to give us with their technology that they think we need, whether we want it or not. In fact, if you keep listening to their words, what these Global Elites have planned gets even worse. Notice what else that doctor said earlier. *"It will allow them to monitor our brains and even mess with and control our thoughts?"*

Wait a second, is that true? Can they really do that? Yes. This is also what we dealt with in great detail in another one of our documentaries called **Hybrids, Super Soldiers & the Coming Genetic Apocalypse.** which again, I encourage you to get.

But there you will see how the governments, military, including DARPA, have been working on this access to our brains for many years now in order to manipulate us. Watch this.

Narrator: *"U.S. President Barak Obama has proposed a $100 million to map the human brain activity in unprecedented detail. Saying this 1.4-kilogram organ remains largely a mystery."*

Barack Obama: *"As humans, we can identify galaxies light-years away. We can study particles smaller than an atom, but we still haven't unlocked the mystery of the three pounds of matter that sits between our ears."*

RT News Reports: *"Back in April of 2013 President Obama unveiled the Brain Initiative, bold new research looking at the brain. The White House pledged to spend $100 million to study how our brains work. One year into the Initiative there's some big news to report. Over the next few months, highly secretive military researchers say they will unveil the enhancement of brain implants, which could one day restore a wounded soldier's memory. The Defense Advanced Research Project Agency, or DARPA, is behind this memory stimulator. While this is great news for those who have suffered brain injury, some people see it in a different light. Manipulating mind memory could open up a minefield.*

There are hundreds upon thousands of agencies in the government. And those agencies usually have agencies within them. And now the Department of Defense has just created a brand new one. This one has a really futuristic name. It's called the Biological Technology Office, or the BTO, and it will cover a lot of amazing programs that would get any Sci-Fi nut excited or scare the living (Bleep) out of an enemy here in the US. It all depends on how you look at it. The new agency reveals its programs coming out of DARPA, which involves living stuff with technology. Something like brain research and synthetic biology.

For instance, they will go over a bunch of programs aimed at understanding the brain in order to develop cybernetic prosthetics. They will actually integrate with the nervous system. So, basically the

*technology will allow the DoD to create Robo-people. The agency will
also work on the technology that will allow humans to control robots
remotely with their minds."*

*ScChannel Reports: "Brain-machine interfaces, a technology that marks
the beginning of the new kind of man, the Cyborg, the Robot man. But as
usual, before there was a man, there was a rat. In this case, a robot rat. A
remote-controlled rat. Neurorobotic technology can be applied in different
directions: the brain controlling the machine or the machine controlling
the brain. Two electrodes in the sensory cortex of the rat send stimuli to
the zone connected to its whiskers. When the rat follows its signals on its
left side and turns in that direction, it is rewarded with a discharge in its
pleasure zone. This discharge releases a flow of dopamine, providing
instant pleasure. This zone is also called the brain's reward center. We
possess a reward center, too, just like the rat. So, it's no coincidence that
these researchers are partly funded by DARPA. Neuroscience will bring
us the soldier of the future. A remote-controlled soldier in the midst of a
battle can be sent crucial data information, downloaded it into his brain.
A soldier who can control his fears and command fire power by thought.
At this stage anything is possible."*

Yeah, including downloading "electronic" information instantly
into our brains to give us a so-called "enhanced" Human 2.0 "upgrade"
like this movie scene shows. Remember this?

*The star, Keanu Reeves, is in a chair and is experiencing excruciating
pain. They are doing something to his brain. Suddenly, he awakens and
the guy controlling the machine looks at him and says, "I think he likes
it." On the screen you can see all the different things they are
downloading into his brain.*

*When he is fully awake, he turns to see Laurence Fishburne sitting next to
him. Reeves turns to him and says, "I know Kung Fu."*

Fishburne replies, "Show me!"

They meet in the workout room and Reeves proceeds to put his newfound knowledge to the test. He performs like a pro until Fishburne catches hold of his foot, spins him around, and Reeves lands on the floor. Fishburne commends his new talent and says, "Good!"

Yeah, good. Wouldn't this be great? To have an instant "enhancement," instant "information" or instant "upgrade?" Well, unfortunately, that movie is one of the many propaganda films that these Global Elites use to condition us into thinking that this new Human 2.0 reality is a good thing for us. And believe it or not, it's a real-life program from DARPA called project TNT, as you can see here in "**DARPA Funds Brain-Stimulation Research to Speed Learning.**"

And just like the doctor said earlier, Elon Musk is right there in the thick of all this Human 2.0 technology and propaganda. He too is trying to get all of us warmed up to the idea that we really should allow these Global Elites access to not just soldier's brains, but even the average Joe's brains. Watch how he puts it here.

Elon Musk: *"I do think that there is a potential path here which is, now I'm really getting into Science Fiction or sort of advanced science stuff. But having some sort of merger with biological intelligence and machine* *intelligence. To some degree we are already a Cyborg. You think of things like the digital tools that you have, your phone, your computer, the applications that you have. Like the fact that I mentioned earlier, you can ask a question and instantly get an answer from Google or other things. And if somebody dies, the digital ghost is still around. All of their emails, the pictures that they posted on social media, that still lives, even if they died.*

So, over time I think we will probably see a closer merger of biological intelligence and digital intelligence. And it's mostly about the bandwidth, the speed of the connection between your brain and your digital extension of yourself. We used to have keyboards that we used a lot and now we do most of our input with our thumbs on a phone, and that is just very slow. A computer can communicate at a rate of a trillion bits per second, but your thumb can, maybe, do 10 bits per second or 100 bits per second if you're being generous. So, some high bandwidth interface to the brain and I think that will be something that helps achieve symbiosis, between human and machine intelligence and maybe solves the control problem and the usefulness problem."

Yahoo Finance Reports: *"Well, Elon Musk's next project isn't a car or a spaceship or a solar panel. The executive's latest start up is called 'Neuralink,' which focuses on the goal of implanting chips into human brains and also connecting brains to computers. Here's what Elon Musk said at a conference in California about the technology last night."*

Elon Musk: *"First, I think it has a very good purpose which is to cure certain diseases and ultimately to help secure humanity's future as a civilization, relative to AI. It has tremendous potential, and we hope to have this in a human patient before the end of next year. It is not far."*

Yahoo Finance Reports: *"'Not far,' he said. The implantation of the neuro-sized thread requires the use of a special robot, but Musk says it's a minimally invasive surgery."*

C/Net Reports: *"Take a look at these other implant technologies. One is called the Utah Array, and the other is the Deep Brain Stimulator. They are very invasive. If you take a look at Neuralink's N1 Sensor, it's tiny. Here it is on a finger, and here it is next to a penny. That's our question. How does one implant something that is so tiny? Build a robot. This is a surgical robot. It feels the complexity of the surgery, such as the subject moving due to breathing. The robot is under the supervision of the surgeon as the electro-threads are implanted. The first product is focused on control. Patients want the ability to control immobile devices with no caretaker necessary. Once that control is possible through the implant, the phone output can be redirected back to a computer as mouse and keyboard inputs.*

Normally, here's how brain surgery goes. Your head may be clamped in place. Your head may be shaved with scarring being a possibility. Neuralink says they want to arrive with something different. They likened it to Lasik, no big scar, no hospital stays. It would be a short procedure and you get to keep all your hair."

Wow! Isn't that special. What a bonus! I get to keep all my hair. But as you can see, even Elon Musk is promoting permanent access to our brain for the purposes of modification with what? An "electronic signal." You know, like a phone or 5G. Go figure. In fact, this ability to, in essence, "hack" the human brain doesn't even require a chip anymore or even Elon Musk's Neuralink procedure. It can also be done, and is already being done, via, wait for it, an "electronic signal." Watch how simple it is to hack the human brain.

Narrator #1: *"It's official! We are living in the future but it's not necessarily, 'Yay! It's all hover boards and robots.' We are living in the 'Oh, no, they could possibly read our minds with technology. Nothing is a secret' future.'"*

Narrator #2: *"Oh, man, I knew we would get here eventually. Hide your brains, kids."*

Narrator #1: *"Scientists have demonstrated how they can hack someone's brain to find out things like numbers, addresses, or whether someone is important to you, to use that against you, like in the CIA movie, to make you talk."*

Narrator #2: *"The craziest thing about all this is that the University of Oxford Geneva in California found a way to pluck this stuff right out of your head with a $300, off-the-shelf, headset. You know, the Epoch headset that lets you control and interact with computers by brainwaves. Computer games through brainwaves. The devices have access to your EEG, which is essentially your electrical brain signal data, which is a neurological phenomenon by your subconscious activity."*

Narrator #1: *"If that isn't creepy enough, they said they can find a person's home 60 percent of the time with a 1 in 10 chance and a 40 percent chance of recognizing the first number of a pin number. Of course, that is only the first number. Now, this is a computer gaming headset. I repeat, a computer gaming headset. And it seems promising when it comes to interrogation in the detection of criminal details."*

With just an "external headset." Imagine what they could do with an internal, programmable computer platform inside of you. You know, like what the people got in the Covid shots. But as you can see, maybe they're trying to cover all bases. I don't know.

But apparently, as wild as it sounds, they don't need a "chip" to gain access to your brain anymore, just an "electronic signal" to do who knows what with. And this is why for years now, for those who have eyes to see and ears to hear, there's been a new term out there floating around called "Brain Hacking." It's a legitimate concern with all this technology, as seen here.

"How Human Brains Could Be Hacked."

In an episode of the Science Channel's "Through the Wormhole," host Morgan Freeman, explores the potential, and dangers, of hacking the mind. (Image credit: <a href="http://www.shutterstock.com/gallery-540794p1.html">Lightspring</a> | <a href="http://www.shutterstock.com/">Shutterstock</a>)

Like computers, human brains may be vulnerable to hackers. Technology is already allowing scientists to read people's thoughts and even plant new ones in the brain.

And that's from Live Science, folks, where they go on to say, *"Like computers, human brains may be vulnerable to hackers. Technology is already allowing scientists to read people's thoughts and even plant new ones in the brain."*

Gee, and this is what they want us to accept as a good thing with this so-called great Human 2.0 technology? I don't think so! They go on to say, *"The latest episode of the Science Channel's 'Through the Wormhole,' hosted by Morgan Freeman, explores the potential — and dangers — of hacking the mind."*

"We live in a world of data," Freeman says in the show. *"One day soon, our innermost thoughts may no longer be our own."*

Well, gee, that's nice. And then another article shares, *"What if the government could change people's moral beliefs or stop political dissent through remote control of people's brains? Sounds like science fiction, right? Well, the government, is very close to accomplishing this."*

That's a direct quote folks, and as scary as that is, giving someone else remote access to your brain and body, it's now being pitched and has been for years as the best idea ever, because it will allow them to create a whole new world free of pain and so-called social equality, you know, Human 2.0. This is what comes with that package. You just use some sort of "electronic signal" that will allow these Global Elites to monitor our education, enhance our education, erase our memories, create new memories for us, give us virtual vacations, allow for a direct reading of our thoughts, determining our thoughts, implanting other thoughts, and even selecting what dreams we want to have via a subscription-based service like Netflix. What are you going to call it? Dreamflix? You think I'm kidding? This is what comes with the new version of humanity called Human 2.0.

Students are in a classroom in China. They each have on a headband. On each of the headbands there is a light that the teacher can see to make sure each student is disciplined in their studies. Red means you're deeply focused. Blue means you're distracted. White means you're offline.

Narrator: *"Teachers at this school in China know exactly when the student isn't paying attention. These headbands measure each student's level of concentration. The information is then directly sent to the teacher by the computer and to the parents. China has big plans to become a global leader in artificial intelligence. It has enabled a cashless economy, where people make purchases with their faces. A giant network of surveillance cameras of facial recognition helps police monitor citizens. Meanwhile some schools offer glimpses of what the future of hi-tech education might look like. The government has poured millions of dollars into the project, bringing together tech giants, start-ups, and schools. We got exclusive access to a school a few hours outside of Shanghai."*

It is morning and the students are out front holding a flag and greeting the people. They all say in unison, "Good morning, everyone."

Narrator: *"We are going to see how high-tech is being used in the classroom. The day begins with the students putting on their brainwave reading gadget. The children meditate. 'Imagine a warm light glowing between your eyebrows.' The device is made in China. It has three electrodes, two behind the ears and one on the forehead. These sensors pick up electrical signals sent by the neurons in the brain. The neuro data is then sent in real time to the computer. So, while students are solving math problems a teacher can quickly find out who is paying attention and who's not."*

Zhu Jiangli, teacher: *"During this period, this student is a bit distracted."* She points to the computer screen showing the data from this particular student.

Narrator: *"A report is then generated to show how well the class is paying attention. It even details each student's concentration level at 10-minute intervals. Its then sent to a chat group for parents. Here you can check every student's score. Classrooms have robots that analyze student's health and engagement level. Students wear uniforms with chips that track their location. There are even surveillance cameras that monitor how often students check their phones or yawn during classes. These gadgets have alarmed Chinese medicine."*

SCI News Reports: *"Our brains are remarkable, miraculous even, but they can't do everything unless you give them a little high-tech help."*

Michio Kaku, theoretical physicist: *"When children see the movie The Matrix, and they see Neo jacking in an electrode and all of a sudden becoming a Kung Fu Master, the first question they ask is, 'How can I get one?' Well, this does not yet exist, but it's actually physically possible. The key to transforming learning from an organ process to a machine-like downloading of information is a squiggly bit of brain known as the hippocampus. The Hippocampus is the gateway to memories. Short term memories are stored right here in the prefrontal cortex, but eventually have to be transferred to long term memories, and that is where the hippocampus comes in."*

Ted Berger: *"This part of the brain doesn't store the memory, but it does the appropriate conversion."*

Narrator: *"At the University of Southern California, bioengineer, Ted Berger, has already proven that a computer chip can replace or enhance brain function. Right now, what our prosthesis does is to convert a code that's kind of in the middle of the hippocampus to what would be the output of the hippocampus."*

Michio Kaku: *"They have been able to take mice and access the electrical signals coursing through the hippocampus and record them. And then when they shot the message back into the hippocampus the mouse remembered the task."*

Ted Berger: *"We found that we can not only restore long-term memories we can enhance the animal's ability to remember. You could think about using devices like this to greatly enhance human memory and to shorten the cycle for learning in terms of downloading huge quantities of memory at a single time."*

Jamais Cascio, Ethical Futurist: *"Chips that augment our hippocampus could very well help us learn faster. So, will that make them a must-have for competitive parents?"*

Michio Kaku*: "At that point it could create an arms race in elementary school. Rumors go out that Jones' kid, he's been enhanced, and our Johnny has to compete with this enhanced kid."*

Jamais Cascio: *"The reality is that with these kinds of technologies, they do not get distributed to everyone at the same time. Some people get it first. Some get it better."*

Jack Uldrich, Global futurist: *"As a society we have to really think long and hard about who gets this. If it's just the wealthy, there are real dangers that they will use it to consolidate their power and their wealth."*

The Doctors TV Show: *"When times get tough, do you wish you could just push that reset button and start all over again? We've all thought about it and wished we could do it from time to time but be careful about what you wish for. Scientists are now working to make these wishes a reality.*

*'It may sound like something out of a Science Fiction film but believe it or not scientists are working on implanting microchips in the human brain to delete memory. Prototypes for the chips are allegedly being tested on

epilepsy patients in hospitals with good results. The creator wants to one day expand this chip not just for the sick but for the healthy population, where users could remove experiences and get this, buy new ones. The chip is predicted to be as common as cell phones in the future. Are you ready?'

There may be a way to get rid of those bad thoughts, fear, or trauma. This whole area of functional brain surgery, whether it be a chip, whether it be brain stimulation. I mean this is an area that is evolving at a crazy rate. I remember when Neal Martin, the neurosurgeon came on and he said, 'Just wait. The time is coming when we are going to be able to control so many of these behaviors, obesity for example.' He said, 'We are going to be able to control it all through the brain.'

This is 'West World-esque,' with someone in the control room somewhere controlling your memories, controlling your thoughts. This is very creepy."

Clip from Total Recall: *Arnold Schwarzenegger gets onboard a train, and the man on the loudspeaker asks, "Do you dream of a vacation at the bottom of the ocean? But you can't float the bill? Have you always wanted to climb the mountains of Mars? But now you are over the hill? Then come to Recall Inc. There you can buy the memory of your ideal vacation. Cheaper, better, and safer than the real thing. So, don't let life pass you by. Call Recall for the memory of a lifetime."*

He proceeds to do just that. He makes his appointment to buy a memory. They prepare to put him into a cylinder when the attendant asks, "Is this your first trip?" He answers, "Yes." They strap down his arms.

He is asked by another attendant, "How do you like your women? Blond, Brunette, Redhead?" He answers, "Brunette." The first attendant says, "Boy, is he going to have a wild time! He's not going to want to come back." Arnold slowly falls to sleep, and they push him into the cylinder.

Julia Sieger, France 24 Reports: *"Can we trust our own brains, and what do our dreams teach us? Is it possible to hack a human brain, and is it as easy as hacking a computer?"*

Moran Cerf, Neuroscientist from Northwestern University: *"It's actually probably easier. The idea is that we are now starting to understand how you can actually influence a person to change their mind and behave a certain way. Companies know how to do that, because this tackles the idea of free will. When Amazon cannot just know what you want but starts offering things that you didn't know that you want, because they know you better than yourself. That's where we are heading. Into a world where your brain is actually the outside world, behind your back."*

Julia Sieger: *"Now you have also studied dreams quite a bit. Can deciphering their meaning be a key to our brains?"*

Moran Cerf: *"Yes, interpreting dreams has been fascinating. We always thought that they meant something. If you don't believe me, you can just tell your husband or your boyfriend in the morning that you dreamed of your ex-boyfriend and see how they respond. They think dreams mean something whether they do or they don't. Now, for the first time in history you can actually access and understand that. During Freud, we had to ask you to tell us what your dream was and believe that this was the story but what they are learning right now is that we can actually get access to your dreams using neuroscience while you are sleeping. The stories that they are telling us is who you are, what you want, what you want to do next and what you think about, all kinds of possibilities. It's needed to understand you better and to control the world around you better. We can also start manipulating your dreams by creating dreams for you, so you can go to sleep and dream a dream that I set up for you. Maybe a filmmaker like Stephen Spielberg could make dreams for people, and so on, or at least you could go to sleep after having a nice evening and continue the evening in your sleep. These companies like Netflix, Hulu, YouTube, Tech24 can put content in and have generally a virtual reality, one that our brains make for us."*

RT.com Reports: *"It's the stuff of a Hollywood movie, but a group of veterans have filed a lawsuit against the CIA and the US Army, claiming that the government implanted remote-controlled devices in their brains. Could this really be happening? Well, joining me to help discuss this is Dr. Colin Ross, president of the Colin A. Ross Institute for Psychological Trauma. Dr. Ross, is this really happening? Did the government really take part in this mind control experiment on soldiers? What kinds of stories have you heard from the survivors of these experiments? I know you have had access to thousands of documents from the CIA.*

Dr. Colin A. Ross: *"Well, there are all types of human experiments where there was no real consent given, and people didn't really know what was going on, and they were basically tricked. Then I think in the brain electrode experiments, it's kind of a combination of both. Some patients were told that the electrodes were being put in their brain for some therapy purpose, when it was really research. Others were told to go here and volunteer when they didn't really have much choice. Others were given a more exact story."*

RT Reports: *"So, what exactly would the government do when they would control someone's minds? What could they make someone do when they manipulated their brain?"*

Colin Ross: *"Well, what is described in the documents, the published papers, is there is an actual photograph of a 16-year-old girl, and she has a series of electrodes in her brain. And, depending on which buttons are being pushed on the transmitter, she is either strumming her guitar, pounding furiously on the wall, or staring off into space. With animals, they are actually directed to walk or swim to a target. So, you can control the actual physical motion and the mental state. How detailed or fine-tuned that's gotten since 1970, again, I don't know; because it's all classified. It must have gotten much more developed."*

RT Reports: *"How fast can this happen? I mean, how fast can a person's mind be taken over? Does it happen over a period of weeks or days?"*

Colin Ross: *"Well, the electrodes are a little different. You can just put the electrode in, you push the button, and it happens."*

You know, you push the button to some sort of "electronic signal" and, voila you can alter a person's brain or body "right away." I wish I was making this up, but let's put all this together. First you get a programmable platform inside of a person, via a chip, a headset, or even an mRNA shot, you know, like in the Covid vaccines, and then with the right "electronic signal" you can begin to manipulate people biologically.

As crazy as all this sounds, remember how the doctor said earlier that this new and improved Human 2.0 future was all laid out by, of all people, Boris Johnson, the Prime Minister of England, in a recent talk he gave to the United Nations? Is that true? Yup. Here it is.

Boris Johnson: *"It's customary for the British Prime Minister to come to the United Nations and pledge to advance our values and defend our rules of a peaceful world and protecting peaceful navigation in the Gulf. To persevering in the vital task of achieving a two-state solution in the conflict in the Middle East and of course I'm proud to do all these things. But no one can ignore a gathering force that is reshaping the future of every member of this assembly. There has been nothing like it in history. When I think of the great scientific revolutions of the past, print, the steam engine, aviation, the atomic age, I think of new tools that we acquired. But over which we, the human race had the advantage, which we controlled and that is not necessarily the case in the digital age.*

You may keep your secrets from your friends, your parents, your children, your doctor, even your personal trainer, but it takes real effort to conceal your thoughts from Google; and, if that is true today, in the future there may be nowhere to hide. Smart cities will populate with sensors all joined together by the internet of things, communing invisibly with lampposts, so there is always a parking space for your electric car. No street will go un-swept, and the urban environment is as antiseptic as the Zurich pharmacy. But this technology could also be used to keep every citizen under round-

the-clock surveillance. A future Alexa will pretend to take orders, but this Alexa will be watching you, clicking her tongue and stamping her foot.

In the future, voice connectivity will be in every room and almost every object. Your mattress will monitor your nightmares, your fridge will beep for more cheese, your front door will sweep wide the moment you approach like some silent butler. Your smart meter will go hustling on its own accord for the cheapest electricity, and every one of them minutely transcribing your every habit in tiny electronic shorthand, stored not in their chips or in their innards. Nowhere you can find it, but in some great cloud of data that glowers evermore oppressively over the human race. A giant, dark thundercloud is waiting to burst, and we have no control over how or when the precipitation will take place. Every day that we tap on our phones or work on our iPads, as I see some of you are doing now, we not only leave our indelible spoor in the ether, but we ourselves are becoming a resource click by click, tap by tap. Just as the Carboniferous period created the indescribable wealth, leaf by decaying leaf of hydrocarbons, data is the crude oil of the modern economy, and we're now in an environment where we don't know who should own these new oil fields. We don't know who should have the rights or the title to these gushers of cash, and we don't know who decides how to use that data and can these algorithms be trusted with our lives and hopes should the machines and only the machines decide whether or not we are eligible for a mortgage or insurance or what surgery or medicines we should receive.

Are we doomed to a cold and heartless future in which the computer says, yes, or the computer says, no, with the grim finality of an emperor in the arena? How do you plead with an algorithm? How do you get it to see extenuating circumstances, and how do we know that the machines have not been insidiously programmed to fool us or even to cheat us? We are already using all kinds of messaging services that offer instant communication at minimal costs, and these same programs, platforms could also be designed for real-time censorship of every conversation with offending words automatically deleted. Indeed, in some countries this happens today. Digital authoritarianism is not alas the stuff of dystopian fantasy but of an emerging reality, and the reason I'm giving this speech today, with this slightly gloomy proem, is that the UK is one of the world's tech leaders and I believe governments have been simply caught unawares by the unintended consequences of the internet, a scientific breakthrough, far more reaching in its everyday psychological impact than any other invention since Gutenberg.

And when you consider how long it took for books to come into widespread circulation, the arrival of the internet is far bigger than print. It's bigger than the Atomic Age, but it's like nuclear power in that it is capable of both good and harm. Of course, it's not alone. As new technologies seem to race towards us from the far horizon, we strain our eyes as they come to make out whether they are for good or bad, friends or foes.

AI. What will it mean? Helpful robots washing and caring for an aging population or pink-eyed Terminators sent back from the future to cull the human race? What will synthetic biology stand for? Restoring our livers and our eyes with miracles, regeneration of the tissues like some fantastic hangover cure or will it bring terrifying limbless chickens to our table? Will nanotechnology help us to beat disease or will it leave tiny robots to replicate in the crevices of ourselves. It is a trope as old as literature, that any scientific advance is punished by the gods."

Actually, "the God," singular, because there's only One. And you wonder why He's coming back to put a stop to all this in what's called "The Seven-Year Tribulation," where He pours out His wrath for seven years, non-stop, and then sets up His righteous reign for 1,000 years to be a true blessing to the human race. The Seven-Year Tribulation is the worst time in the history of mankind. You don't want to be there.

Matthew 24:21-22 "For then there will be great distress, unequaled from the beginning of the world until now – and never to be equaled again. If those days had not been cut short, no one would survive."

That's from Jesus folks. You really need to heed His warning and get saved through Him before it's too late. Receive His mercy, not His wrath. But again, what you just saw was the actual video of Boris Johnson in front of the United Nations telling us what's coming with this Human 2.0 future that's being built for us, whether we want it or not. And by the way, he thinks it's a good thing, if you watch the rest of his speech, which is crazy. Even after exposing the dangers, he still thinks it's the way of the future for all of us. But that doesn't sound like a good future to me. How about you? I think I'll stick with the Human Original 1.0., i.e., God's design!

But let's continue, as wild as all this is. That doctor in the interview also said that this type of Electronic Global connected system, Human 2.0, was already being given a trial run by Bill Gates in West Africa. Now, is that true? Yes. It's in the news if you've got eyes to see and ears to hear!

"Africa to Become Test Bed for Gates Funded Biometric ID System."

And it will hold information like your vaccination status as seen here.

'Gates-funded Program to Begin Tests on Biometric ID Vaccination Records in Africa."

And that will determine your ability to financially interact in the world as seen here.

"Africa to Become Testing Ground for 'Trust Stamp' Vaccine Record and Payment System."

Gates-funded Program to Begin Tests on Biometric ID Vaccination Records in Africa

The biometric digital identity platform Trust Stamp, which claims to 'evolve as you evolve " is to be introduced in 'low-income, remote communities' in West Africa as part of a partnership between the Bill Gates-supported GAVI vaccine alliance and Mastercard.

According to a probe by Mastercard, Trust Stamp uses biometrics to verify your identity without revealing any information.

"A biometric digital identity platform that 'evolves just as you evolve' is set to be introduced in 'low-income, remote communities' in West Africa."

"Thanks to a public-private partnership between the Bill Gates-backed GAVI, or "Global Alliance for Vaccines and Immunization,' Mastercard, and the AI-powered 'identity authentication' company, Trust Stamp."

"The program, which was first launched in late 2018, will see Trust Stamp's digital identity platform integrated into the GAVI-Mastercard 'Wellness Pass,' a digital vaccination record and identity system that is also linked to Mastercard's click-to-play system that is powered by its AI and machine-learning technology, called NuData."

"Mastercard, in addition to professing its commitment to promoting 'centralized record keeping of childhood immunization' also described as a leader toward a 'World Beyond Cash,' and its partnership with GAVI, marks a novel approach towards linking a biometric digital identity

system, vaccination records, and a payment system into a single cohesive platform."

"The effort, since its launch nearly two years ago, has been funded via $3.8 million in GAVI donor funds, in addition to a matched donation of the same amount by the Bill and Melinda Gates Foundation."

"In early June, GAVI reported that Mastercard's Wellness Pass program would be adapted in response to the coronavirus (COVID-19) pandemic and that Trust Stamp's biometric identity platform would be integrated into Wellness Pass as Trust Stamp's system."

"Trust Stamp's interest in providing its technology to both COVID-19 response and to law enforcement is part of a growing trend where numerous companies providing digital solutions to COVID-19 also offer the same solutions to prison systems and law enforcement for the purposes of surveillance and 'predictive policing.'"

You know, like what's going on inside your head as well as the data retrieved from you continually, non-stop, as you're continually being tracked like a rat and monitored endlessly, including your behavior and thoughts in this new Human 2.0. system. It will apparently even allow them to "predict" what you'll do next. Which is what that term means, "predictive policing." That's coming with their plan as well. But the article goes on to say, *"West Africa is just the test bed. They plan on doing this to the whole world and with their newly installed global monitoring system with 5G and the programmable computer interface they've now got inside of people, which will allow them to monitor all people at all times, in what's being called Smart Cities, where everyone and everything is 'electronically' connected, so they can implement a Smart Social Credit System."*

In other words, what the Bible calls the Mark of the Beast system that will control what people around the whole world can "buy or sell" based on their "approved" behavior. Their Human 2.0 system sounds eerily familiar to what the Bible says is coming in the Seven-Year Tribulation.

Revelation 13:16-17 "He also forced everyone, small and great, rich, and poor, free and slave, to receive a mark on his right hand or on his forehead, so that no one could buy or sell unless he had the mark, which is the name of the beast or the number of his name."

This "marking system" that controls people's "buying and selling" on a global basis is what the Bible calls the Mark of the Beast system, and it's not good. It also sounds a whole lot like what that doctor said earlier was coming, and what Boris Johnson described, and is what is already well underway in China, of all places. Here's what's coming to the whole world if these Global Elites get their way.

Narrator: *"Throughout the annals of science fiction, the future cities are basically dystopias. Think of the bleak lives of city dwellers in 'Blade Runner,' 'Metropolis,' or 'The Caves of Steel.' Recent projections show that by 2050, two-thirds of the global population will live in cities, which makes it imperative that our vast urban cities aren't health-scapes but instead are smart urban centers with a dash of Sci-Fi, devices, roads, and lampposts, all talking to each other. They can make cities safer and smoother. This transformation is already beginning.*

A smart city is where items around town are connected. Streets, buildings, personal devices, cars, power grids, all sending data back and forth, passively working together to improve the community. Imagine public buses that trigger sensors in the road, providing a real time ETA. Streetlights that dim or brighten, depending on foot traffic. Stop lights warning of an accident ahead. At the core, a smart city are two things: sensors to collect data and the connectivity to send and receive it. Some cities were early on the connectivity part, like Barcelona, which has had fiberoptic cables embedded below its streets for more than 30 years.

Meanwhile sensors have become smaller, cheaper, and more powerful, giving rise to the internet. It's no wonder that the number of connected devices jumped to 8.4 billion in 2017, an increase of one-third in a single year. With these two major technological features in place, spots around the globe are launching large scale smart city projects. In Barcelona, sensor-imbedded parking spots connect with an app that directs drivers to available spaces. Streetlamps brighten automatically, and they are part of Barcelona's Wi-Fi network, providing free internet access across the city.

Similar smart city projects are underway in Stockholm, Amsterdam, Copenhagen, and Columbus, Ohio. Some focusing on energy usage, others on safety and public transportation, but all hoping to make their cities that much better."

"Nobody does authoritarianism quite like China. By 2020 every citizen will have a social credit score that will go up and down based on their personal behavior. Bad behavior leading to a reduction in credit will include jaywalking."

As the man steps out into the street to proceed to jaywalk a voice comes on from a speaker behind him. "You are illegally crossing this road. Stand back!" So, very quickly he turns around and steps back onto the sidewalk.

"Bad driving, smoking on trains."

While the train is moving a voice comes on the intercom saying, "Dear passengers, people who travel without a ticket or behave disorderly or smoke in public areas will be punished according to regulations and the behavior will be recorded in the individual credit information system. To avoid a negative record of personal credit please follow the relevant regulations."

"Buying too many video games, buying too much junk food, buying too much alcohol, calling a friend who has a too low of a credit score, merely having a friend online who has a low credit score, posting fake news online, criticizing the government, having an unauthorized website, walking a dog without a leash, letting your dog bark too much. Back in 1984, Winston Smith could take a train to temporarily escape the

surveillance state. In China, low rank citizens will be prevented from taking buses, planes, and trains."

Citizen of China: *"Right now my ability to travel is limited."*

"Now, where have I seen that before?"

A clip from "Black Mirror." *A lady has come up to the counter to get a ticket to board a plane. The person behind the counter tells her, "That is reserved for the members of our prime-flight program. You have to be a full-time member to qualify." The lady trying to buy a ticket says, "Oh, I'm a prime-flight member." But the person behind the counter, shakes her head and points to a screen on the counter and says, "No. This shows you are a 183." But the lady replies, "No, that was when I called someone down in the ..." The person behind the counter replies, "I'm sorry can I book you another connection?"*

"6.7 million Chinese people have already been prevented from buying airline and train tickets. The punishments for citizens who have a credit score that sinks too low are limited only by the imagination. When renting a home, obtaining a loan, booking a hotel, filling the car with petrol, all will be restricted."

Chinese citizen: *"I can't buy property, my child can't go to private school, you feel like you are being controlled by the government all the time."*

"The entire system will be up with an estimated 400 million surveillance cameras with facial recognition software. Cameras at intersections will zero in on their face and publicly shame them on nearby video screens."

"It will eventually encompass the real time location, tracking citizens by their cell phones. Overall credit scores can go up and down in real time based on a person's behavior. They can also be affected by the people they associate with, and all this will be unified in a centralized database. In the words of the Chinese Government..."

Chinese Government: *"If trust is broken in one place, restrictions are imposed everywhere."*

"They literally say if those deemed untrustworthy, they will be unable to move even a single step."

Chinese official: *"Our goal is to ensure that if people keep their promises they can go anywhere in the world; and if they break their promises, they won't be able to move an inch."*

"Who cares about what's happening in China, right? It's not like they are selling the same technologies to be used in the West. Do you think that a social credit score could ever happen over here? Well, think again because there already is, thanks to Silicon Valley. People are already losing their public square platform for their dissenting opinions. People's trustworthiness is already being ranked by social media giants, depending on what links they post. People are already being refused bank accounts, eCommerce, and the ability to raise money for expressing controversial ideas. Imagine going to buy groceries with your credit card and then someone in an office somewhere in San Francisco deemed something you posted on the internet to be hateful, and your transaction is declined. You can forget even trying to pay, because your implanted microchip will be blocked so you won't even be able to enter the shop."

Wow! Doesn't that sound great? Actually, it sounds like a horrible nightmare. A life of constant monitoring, constant control, and constant manipulation like a rat in a cage. This is Human 2.0 folks. And they won't just know what posts you put up online, they have plans of even knowing what's going on in your own mind, i.e., total thought control. George Orwell, eat your heart out. This is making what he envisioned look like chump change!

And notice how Artificial Intelligence, or AI, is how they're going to be pulling all of this global monitoring infrastructure off, which is obviously way too big for humans to handle. Therefore, you need something superhuman, which is where AI comes in and which is why AI s also a huge part of the World Economic Forum's vision of our future, as seen again on their 5G global map right next to Retail, Consumer Goods & Lifestyle. You know, the "buying and selling" aspect. And I would encourage you to also get yourself equipped on that issue with another study we have called *"The AI Invasion."*

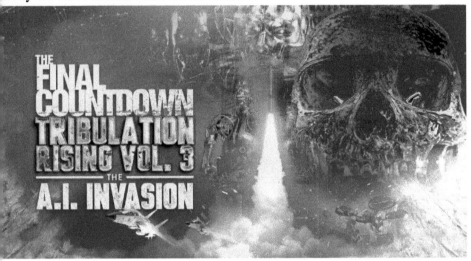

AI isn't just coming, it's already here in many forms, and it's already taking over virtually everything on the planet, just in time for these Global Elites to implement their plans for Human 2.0.

In fact, another one of their researchers also admitted that once we give access to these Global Elites via the "electronic matrix system" that's being built for us, which links our brains and bodies to it, and once we allow AI to control it and monitor it all on a global basis, it will "not" lead to Utopia as they would have us believe; but, rather, some pretty freaky, nightmarish problems that we can't even dream of or have ever even thought of before.

TEDXCEIBS conference: *"For the future of the brain, our human brain and where it is headed with technology. Right now, scientists in laboratories around the world are developing brain chips. These are chips that can be inserted into the brain, and they are wireless. We will have* *brain chips in humans, and the people who will get these brain chips first are people who suffer from severe medical conditions. So, if you have a severe medical condition, like you are paralyzed from the neck down, or you suffer from a brain disorder, like Alzheimer's disease or Parkinson's disease, that brain chip can restore your quality of life.*

Would you hesitate to get the chip? Of course not. You would say put that chip in my brain. Mind to mind communication, this is something of science fiction that we all read about. But this is actually possible today. As I just showed you. So, there will come a point where if we have a chip in our brain, and you out there have a chip in your brain, we can communicate. We can communicate without talking, we can communicate when you are halfway around the world. And we can exchange knowledge.

So, if you look at a world where we have a chip that is connected to the internet, all of a sudden, every piece of information on the internet becomes accessible to our minds. Now, when we look back at today and we have to go to Google and type it in, that would be so primitive. Nobody will do that. You will just think, what knowledge do I need? And it will appear there for you to use.

But it gets even weirder, stranger, because we will not only be able to transfer knowledge, but we will be able to transfer memories. Now, you could have an experience, like skydiving and all of a sudden, you could transfer that experience to a friend; and all of a sudden, they have that experience with what you have experienced. It gets even weirder, because we will be living our lives as our lives, we know our lives in our memories, but you will also have access to anybody's life that wants to make it available to you.

All of us are learning here at CEIBS getting our EMBAs and MBAs. Well, this will be obsolete, because CEIBS will literally be in the Cloud; and you will just download from the best minds in the world, whatever you need to know, when you need to know it. We will no longer have Universities as we have them today. Things will change. Information will be on demand. Information will be commoditized. Knowledge will be commoditized. All of us will be smarter, have an infinite amount of storage and infinite access to information. It will be unheard of. We will no longer be this isolated human being. We will be connected to everything, and when we do that, we have to understand that this is a big responsibility.

It's something that we as a society, we as a human race, must think about very, very carefully. Imagine, people could hack your cell phone, people could hack your computer, and it could be bad. They could steal your banking information, take all your money. They could steal your identity, but they can't really hurt you. In the future, if somebody hacks into your head because you are connected to the internet, they can steal you. They could actually steal you. They could implant memories into your head that you don't have. They could erase memories. They could control you in ways that you wouldn't even know you were being controlled. Is this scary?"

Uh yeah, just a wee bit there! And you might be thinking, "Well that's precisely why I'm not going to get one of those brain chips he was talking about. I don't care how many times Elon Musk and the other Global Elites encourage us to do so." Well, that's the question. Did you get the jab? Remember, that contained a "computing system" as well.

But you might also be thinking, "Okay, wait a second, wait a second! This is a total violation of our human rights! They can't do this to us…to people. We're humans, not cattle!"

Well, I would agree, but apparently these Global Elites disagree. Believe it or not, they believe that they have a "legal" work-around to this "human" violation. They believe they now have "legal" justification for treating us like cattle, and that's because they say they can "legally violate" our "human" rights because we chose to inject ourselves with a non-human "synthetic" material called mRNA in the vaccines. You know, the programmable computer interface. And they say, because of this, legally, according to their definition anyway, this makes us no longer "human."

So now, we've become just a bunch of cattle who have no "human" rights. In fact, for those who got the shots they say they shouldn't be classified as "humans" anymore. Rather, they have become "animals" by definition that have no rights. Now, as insane as this sounds, this is yet another thing Todd Callender brought out in another interview he gave.

TruNews: *"The shareholder of the messenger of the mRNA could legally claim ownership of human beings."*

Todd Callender: *"Yes, except that they are not human beings. This is the issue. They are a synthetic genome. They are a new species. In fact, they have already named the species. They call them Homo bodoensis. You and I are Homo sapien. And what is homicide? Homicide is the unlawful taking of a human being. How do you describe a human being? It's Homo sapien. So, what happens when you kill somebody that is Homo bodoensis, not a Homo-sapien? Is there a crime committed? When you shoot your dog in the head, did you commit homicide? No! It's a dog, not a human. This is my concern as to where this goes. Do you want to talk about a slippery slope?"*

Trunews Reports: *So, you can declare a massive portion of the human population is non-human."*

Todd Callender: *"That's right!"*

Boy, did we get fooled. At least those who got the shots. Apparently, the term Human 2.0 really does mean "human cattle" or "no longer human," and that becomes their "legal justification" for treating us just like animals! This is sick, folks!

Chapter Six

The Resisters of Human 2.0

But wait a second. What about the resisters? Because you know there's going to be a whole lot of resisters to being treated as cattle. I mean, personally, I'm not going to go along with this. And when other people find out what they're really up to, which again, is why we're doing publishing this, then I think they'll resist too. What will they do with those folks? Well, let's go back to Todd Callender's last statement we saw in the last clip from The Corona Investigative Committee. I think we'll find the answer to what the Global Elites do with those who resist their creation of Human 2.0.

Quote, *"Is the Government really looking at using this 'next created crisis' as an excuse to implement Marshall Law and put people into quarantine centers and FEMA camps? And were these 'advanced plans' outlined with something called The Marburg Provisions Prep Act?"*

Unfortunately, the answer is yes! All of this stated there is yes. But don't take my word for it. Let's listen to the CDC, the Center for Disease Control. They even admit they're going to be putting people into "camps" and still to this day have it proudly displayed on their website, as you can see here. It's called the **"Shielding Approach,"** because you just don't tell people you're going to put them into camps. No, they'll freak out. So, you call it the "**Shielding Approach**" and the creation of "**Green Zones,**" which is a more palatable way of saying, "We're going to haul you off, right out of your own house, and throw you into a camp just like the Germans did with the Jewish people."

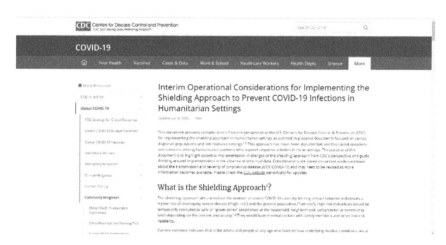

As crazy as that sounds, and I quote: *"The shielding approach aims to reduce the number of severe COVID-19 cases by limiting contact between individuals at higher risk of developing severe disease ("high-risk") and the general population ("low-risk"). High-risk individuals would be temporarily relocated to safe or "green zones" established at the household, neighborhood, camp/sector, or community level depending on the context and setting. They would have minimal contact*

with family members and other low-risk residents."

In other words, they will haul you off to a camp like the Jews. I wonder if they'll use trains to transfer people too. But you might be thinking, "Come on now. They aren't really building camps all over the world to haul people away against their own will, just like what Hitler did to the Jewish people in Germany, who were also considered "unclean" in society, as well, are they?"

Unfortunately, they already "have,", and they already "are" throwing people into these camps, as seen here.

Newscaster: *"The Chinese government collected an excessive amount of data about their citizens, and they are using it in novel ways to tackle the coronavirus. Every time she wants to leave her apartment, she has to scan* *her face and load images, as well as images from all their CCT cameras in China of which there are about 200 million fed into a central database and then analyzed using machine learning. So, basically, if you are in sight of a camera, there's about five on this crossroads, then it's like the Chinese government has analyzed your face and know where you are.*

Another source of data is the WeChat app. You might have heard of it. WeChat is social media and your debit card all rolled into one super app which is really convenient. It also knows where you are and what you are saying to friends. That is what the state is doing, and the Chinese people generally know about this. The images you see are actually from the state media. But they are using this data to try the highest tech academic control ever attempted.

If you go to the hospital, the hospital will register with the authorities and the authorities will pull your name down from their database and they have an algorithm that will tell them all the different places you have been in the last 14 days and all the people that you might have been in contact with. So, the bread that you bought with the WeChat app, the baker now will be notified that they have to self-quarantine for 14 days and the people you were next to on the flight, they now have to self-isolate for the next 14 days. Every single citizen has a code red, amber or green.

Chinese citizen: *"I guess you're yellow."*

Newscaster: *"Why?" Automatic color coding determines where you can go.*

Chinese citizen: *"Why? Because you come to Shanghai and hadn't had 14 days. I'm green. I'm safe."*

Newscaster: *"If I'm yellow, shouldn't you be yellow?"*

Chinese citizen: *"No, just you. Maybe next week you are going to be green. In some cities you cannot drive on the road, if you are not green. If you are the other colors, you can't drive."*

Newscaster: *"This does seem to be working, because you can identify and contain hotspots before they get out of control. It means that people can continue working if they're not a risk of contamination and then self-isolate if they are.*

We are in Shanghai, which is about 100 kilometers away from Wuhan. This place has been locked down for months now. This is beginning to come back to life a bit. Your temperature is checked entering most buildings. This last time I was here, there was basically no one here. The stores are beginning to open up a bit. Generally, you are not allowed to eat in the restaurants. You are allowed to buy take away, but you are not allowed to sit down and eat.

We are now in a Tai Chi studio."

Wuming, Tai Chi teacher: *"I am a Tai Chi teacher. This is my Tai Chi school. Because of the virus we can't teach our students. I don't know when we will be able to open the door and welcome back my students. Maybe next month. So, I wait until somebody tells me."*

Newscaster: *"This crisis has been a massive cost to the Chinese economy. They had taken a hit early on. But things are beginning to open now in most of the country. Every single person that comes into China now has to self-quarantine for 14 days. So, every day I have to fill in this graph with my temperature. Many flights coming into the country are screened. We've been waiting in Shanghai airport for about two hours now. We'll get there eventually.*

Only one person from each household can go out every three days to buy essentials. Hubei has also banned all vehicles from the road. You can only drive with a special permit. So, complete lockdown, tracing those with the virus with big data and the glue that holds it all together is the intense promotion of social solidarity. The Government has framed this as a people's war against the virus. These messages of solidarity are all over social media and big advertisements on the street."

Lady on the street as she is looking at one of the signs says, "Go China! We do it!"

Newscaster*: "The academia requires collective action and personal sacrifice, like no panic buying and staying at home when you are told to. The Chinese government has tools like these street signs in every public space as well as controlling social media. The Chinese populace has complied with the requirements to control the virus."*

But what if you don't comply??

One India Reports: *"China is taking severe measures to combat the Covid-19 virus, and the country prepares to host the Winter Olympics in a month. Amid a surge in cases, China is reportedly putting suspected Covid-19 patients in metal boxes to prevent the spread of the disease per its zero Covid policies. It was reported that people, including pregnant women and children and elderly, are forced to stay in these cramped boxes with a wooden bed and a toilet for as long as two weeks, even if a single person tests positive in their locality. Various videos shown on Chinese social media show the chaotic scenes. Some families have to pack up overnight to be sent to quarantine centers. Long lines of buses can be seen on the street that are taking people to Covid-19 quarantine camps. Here is a notice to Tianjin City."*

Authority is busy ending tens of thousands of people off to Covid quarantine camps with hundreds of buses now. Only one Covid case found in your apartment building, all residents of your building will be sent off to Covid quarantine camps. 2022/1/10

At least 20 million people are now confined to their homes in China and cannot leave their homes even to buy food, according to the report. China enforces its lockdowns and quarantine measures with an iron hand."

NDTV reports: *People are forced to quarantine in tiny metal boxes under China's zero Covid rule. Rows upon rows of metal boxes to house suspected Covid-19 patients seen in nightmarish social media videos from*

China. China has imposed several draconian rules on its citizens under its 'Zero Covid' policy. People are being forced to stay in these crammed boxes furnished with a wooden bed and a toilet for as long as two weeks. Pregnant women and children are believed to be among those sent to these camps. Some residents were told just after midnight that they need to leave their homes and go to the quarantine centers."

Russell Brand: *"What is happening in Australia? When did we start to examine the human rights angle here by consent of the government?"*

Australian Lady: *"It's horrible. It's a horrible feeling. You feel like you are in prison. You feel like you have done something wrong. It's inhumane what they are doing. You are so small, and they just overpower you and you are literally nothing. It's like, 'You do what we say, or you're in trouble and we will lock you up longer.' They would be threatening me, if I were to do this again. 'We will extend your time in here.'"*

UnHerd reports of conditions in camp. A man is standing outside of a window all dressed in white. A lady in the room they are quarantined in is asking him if she can just go do the laundry.

Man in White: *"You're allowed to go to the laundry, but you've got to wear a mask. And you definitely can't go up the fencing rails. But you're allowed to go to the laundry, yeah? That's always been the case."*

Lady on the porch: *"If I were sitting right here, right near the fence? Why do they have a cabin right near the fence? It makes no sense, does it?*

Man in White: *"Yeah, but you can't leave your balcony to go to the fence to talk to somebody else. That's just obvious. Again, it doesn't have to make sense. There has to be lines everywhere drawn, yeah? And one of the lines is you cannot leave your balcony, and you cannot go to someone else. When it makes no sense or doesn't seem right to you. That is the line and that is what the law says here, and that's how it goes. Yep, there's a CHO direction on how the behavior must be done, especially in this area;*

because it's much more highly infectious and likely to have infected people here."

Lady on the porch: *"All the highly infectious when all of us are negative."*

Man in White: *"So far, the risk is still very high."*

9News Reports: *"Good morning, we start with breaking news where three people have escaped from the Howard Springs Covid facility. Talia Savage is there for a report. Talia, good morning. There is a search going on right now?"*

Talia Savage: *"That's right, we have been told that the search began about 4:40 am this morning. Checkpoints have been set up around Howard Springs for the past several hours. As you can see, they are conducting thorough searches of cars, checking vehicle registrations, cars, and buses alike."*

Tucker Carlson: *"What if your next-door neighbor suddenly went dangerously insane and started holding people hostage in his house. Would you consider that threatening? Would you even notice it? Those are not just theoretical questions. Something like that just happened in our national neighborhood. Canada, the land mass directly to our north, who is our largest trading partner, who we share the longest international border in the world, Canada took a dramatic move, took the legitimately dangerous move to authoritarianism. In Canada, yes!*

Here's just one measure of it. On Monday, the country's Prime Minister Trudeau, outlined his country's corona regulations. Canadians hoping to return to their country must be tested before and after takeoff he said. Quote:

'If your results come back negative for Covid-19, you'll be able to head home and finish your mandatory quarantine there. If your test results

come back positive, you'll need to immediately quarantine in designated government facilities. This is not optional.'

Designated government facilities. Now, when this happens in other countries, as it does, we call these facilities internment camps. But because this is Canada we are talking about, the place where we assumed was passive and polite and Anglo to the point of parody, no one thinks to use that term. In fact, no one thinks about it at all. Trudeau's internment policy has been in place since last month, and as far as we can tell, no major U.S network has even mentioned it. And neither has our State Department, which ordinarily seems to exist to make unhappy noises about human rights violations around the world. But not a word about Canada.

Preconceptions may play some role here. We assume that interning people is what Russia does. Boarding people is what Canada does. But not anymore. Suddenly Canada is a flagrant violator of basic human rights. If you fail a Covid test, they will lock you up without a trial. And go ahead and try to disobey. According to the Canadian government, anyone who attempts to avoid these rules, detention in a government internment facility, for example, could face a million-dollar fine and three years in prison. This is Justin Trudeau's Canada. It's funny, Trudeau always seemed like a cheerful idiot wearing weird costumes and yammering on about diversity. Who knew he was Mussolini?

There might be a lesson here for other nations that are led by shallow, neo-liberal, empty suits. Know any? Underneath all the chirping identity politics talk, it's not a joke. It's internment cells. In Canada, where everything has a euphemism, those cells are referred to as approved quarantine hotels. What are they like? Well, as noted, they are internment cells. What do you think they are like? There are shortages of food and water, or you could be sexually assaulted as you are held in one. Listen to a member of the Canadian Parliament explain what they are like.

'The liberals instituted a Federal Hotel Quarantine requirement for those entering Canada. We have heard reports that it's taking hours to book *these hotels, dietary restrictions are not being met, and food and water are not always readily available. That's in addition to this program continuing after reports of sexual assault. This is mind-boggling.'*

Oh, the liberals did this. Suffering liberals to intern people, is it? According to a post in the 'Post Millennial,' the doors in many of the internment facilities don't lock, and the detainees have no way to protect themselves while they sleep, hint the sex assault. They also don't have access to medical care. In one case, the authorities detained a man with diabetes, called Ray Truesdale. What was Truesdale's crime?

Well, he was flying from Tennessee to Toronto on a business trip. As he waited in confinement for his corona test results, his jailers forgot to feed Truesdale for more than 24 hours. Ultimately, Truesdale went downstairs in search of something to eat. There he found others that were held without food. They were screaming, he said. In the end the authorities informed Truesdale that his corona sample had been damaged somehow so he had to remain in internment.

Well, consider Mitch Beaulieu, a Canadian who landed in Calgary after a business trip to Florida. He told Canadian television that his experience was very much like a kidnapping. I quote:

'I was put in a black van with tinted windows and taken to an undisclosed location. I was like 'Where am I going. Why am I going there? They were like, 'We'll tell you everything when you get there' ... I thought I was being punked. But I wasn't. Where are the hidden cameras? I got out there and there was plastic all over, people walking around in ... hazmat suits ... it was like jail pretty much.'

Yeah, just don't call it a jail. And that is an order directly from Canadian state media. This fall, the CBC media ran a story with this headline, 'PM, health officials warn Canadians against believing Covid-19 internment camps disinformation.' Warned them against believing. Sounds familiar. That claim, that conspiracy theory; 'The claim that the federal government is preparing to forcibly intern Canadians is patently false.'

The CBC assured Canadians that the government was preparing 'voluntary quarantine sites.'

Yes, voluntary in the sense of being mandatory, which is what they are; they are mandatory. What is so interesting is that Canada's new rule only applies to Covid patients. Other transmissible diseases are exempt. People with AIDS aren't being sent to internment facilities, thank God. No one has tried to do that since Fidel Castro did it in the 1980's. Drug resistant TB is fine. It's a real problem, but not in Canada. Only Covid with a 98 percent survival rate."

WION News Reports: *"Its probably the biggest quarantine in human history. Millions of people are in a state of lockdown in China. Even outside mainland China, there are thousands of people worldwide who are being quarantined. Let's take a look at what life is like inside quarantine camps from Serbia to Australia to the United States."*

Did he just say the United States? I mean, it's one thing in China, Australia, Canada, Europe, and other regions, but even here? Yes, the CDC told you that's exactly what they're going to do! It's still on their website. And if this is all starting to sound familiar, it is. How is it any different, and how is it not the same rationale and scenario of these camps that were created for "people's safety" and the "well-being" of society?

Narrator showing clips of concentration camp: *"These aerial pictures taken a few days ago gives you some idea of this place. Twenty-eight brick buildings, with each housing over a thousand prisoners. Nearby the family residence of the notorious Commandant Rudolph Hess, the man who oversaw the death of more than a million people. A mile or so away is Auschwitz 2, 25 times bigger and built from scratch to facilitate mass murder on an industrial scale. Many of the wood or brick-built blocks were destroyed before the Nazis fled, and the railway ramps, where Nazi doctors examined arriving prisoners, deciding on the strong, who should live and the weak, often children, who were taken off to the gas chambers.*

You know, who's got Covid and who doesn't, something that has over a 98% survivability rate, makes about as much sense, doesn't it? It's all insane murderous behavior. And if it was wrong then, it's wrong today! But hey, good thing that's not coming here to America. Unfortunately, it already has, as seen here.

Stew Peters: *"Nearly two years into this pandemic, if there is one question that remains crucial and is still officially unanswered was this pandemic really an accident or was it planned by someone, somewhere, for some specific nefarious purpose? We think we know the answer and so does British Funeral Director, John O'Looney. He believes that he saw the plan for the pandemic, well under way, even before Covid-19 ever emerged. He also has a fascinating theory about the real intent of the Covid-19 shots. He joined us, and that interview went viral. Here is what he said.*

So, yesterday on this program, Karen Kingston, joined us. She worked for Pfizer years ago. She's a biotech analyst, and she said if kids become injected, she just doesn't know how they will survive. Do you agree with that sentiment?

John O'Looney: *"100 percent. I've agreed with it before, and I agree with it now. On Tuesday I went for a meeting in London, and we sat with a very eminent member of Parliament, very influential. I'm going to resist naming him, but I was surrounded by a plethora of the very brightest, scientific, and legal minds in the world. One was Dolores Cahill, who has run level three biolabs and has worked in level four, and a plethora of others. I could have a list and read them all up there. They are household names because of their expertise.*

They basically said that they foresee in October, November, and December a terrible death rate, globally, exclusively in the vaccinated. Children that are injected will die. The main causes of this will be inflammation of the heart, and that has been well-documented but ignored constantly. Those deaths will be labeled swiftly as a new virulent strain of Covid. Let me be very clear in doing that, because every few weeks you have a new strain. 'There's a new variant. There's a new variant,' and this variant is said to do the most damage.' Now there will be civil unrest as people slowly come to terms that they have been lied to. Nobody loves anything more than their kids. It doesn't matter who you are, where you come from, what country or faith, religion; we love our kids more than anything else in the world. And when these people that have been duped take their kids for the injection and their kids die, they won't go for the variant story.

And that is exactly what they want. So, that's the excuse they need, then they can launch Marshall Law. Once they bring in Marshall Law, they will go door-to-door then force vaccination or take people off to internment camps. That is what will happen. I have spoken in depth with these brilliant minds and the feeling, the consensus, is this is what is going to happen, unless we can turn it around and convince these advocates that they've been lied to and to encourage them to look at the scientific data. We spoke to this guy, and he wasn't remotely surprised. He knew. He knew, and he couldn't give any guarantees, but he said he would see what he could do. I need to speak out and tell people they need to wake up. If they don't, very surely, you will be sitting in your house and look out your window and you are going to see police taking people away.

You are going to see them as a deadly threat, because you will be sick and dying and you will be happy for that threat to be removed. It's all part of a well-orchestrated, well-funded, elaborate lie."

Stew Peters: *"Well let's talk about these internment camps a little bit. You said there are satellite images."*

John O'Looney: *"Yes, the one that's closest to me is obviously the one I am focused on here in Australia. A number of Australians, thousands of Australians, I've taken thousands of calls and emails, obviously since going public, more than I could ever answer. I would hasten to answer, my apologies, if you haven't heard back from me. I can assure you, I'm real. This is me. Pressure has been put on me already. Now I'm a 53-year-old guy. I've grown up with the constant specter of prison overcrowding.*

Sometimes it was more of an advertisement. Every now and again we would get a new Secretary who promises to address this, and they never do. I can remember the last time one was elected to power, and he made promises and he kept them. Then he was robbed in the last American election. I genuinely believe that people just don't keep their promises.

Why do they feel the need to build these superstructures now? At a time when the world is on its knees economically. Actually, build these facilities. What are they for? What is the need for them? Does this detract from what I am saying? Does it give credence to what I am saying? And any question you could ask me, I have an answer for."

Stew Peters: *"Here in the United States they have CDC green zones. The Center for Disease Control has actually published these green zones that are supposed to be safe for people to go who have not been inoculated or have been jabbed or have Covid or have antibodies. I don't know. Whatever it is, they published this on their website. And this is just a way to segregate one class of people from another. People who have been jabbed, people who haven't, people who are sick with covid, people who are not, people who have symptoms. What do you suppose that keeps this mass amount of people from understanding actual data?"*

John O'Looney: *"Trusting government, trusting in the propaganda that's been spewed out consistently."*

Next interview:

Stew Peters: *"So you have learned about a $1.3-billion budget that has been allocated to prison camps. What is this?*

Maria Zeee*: "Correct. Because when we were supposedly done with Covid, we are supposedly learning to live with the virus, as you and I spoke about some time ago, yet they were planning on expanding these camps. And at the time we discovered some more camps, and now they are allocating the sum of 1.3 billion to expand and build more of these. And some of these are in locations where they had previously dumped military* *waste, so they are not actually safe for people. What do we need $1.3 billion for, to continue to expand these things? Other than if they are going to be used for dissent, which is what I am becoming increasingly convinced of, Stew."*

Stew Peters: *"Yes, there is evidence of this all over the place. We just spoke to a January 6th defendant. This was somebody that showed dissent against the stolen election, a Marxist coup that took place in this country. Didn't have a weapon, didn't infiltrate and cause damage, or assault, cause damage, or rape anyone. He was there as a journalist to take photographs and document the occurrences and the event of the day and is looking at up to 20 years in prison. Having to crowdfund to raise money for his family in case he is gone for two decades. His kids, when he gets out of prison, his kids will be grownups. This is insanity what is happening in this world. And it's not just exclusive in the United States. These governments are horrifyingly in lockstep, including Down Under, which up until recently was primarily an English-speaking democracy of sorts, set up similar to here in the United States, and is now seemingly going back to the original prison colony, as it was founded as."*

And so are massive amounts of other countries with Covid with the excuse as to why we need to hurry up and build these "camps," I mean "safe zones," all over the place. $1.3 billion …wow…that's a lot of money just from that one government. But they're not alone. What are they going to do with all that financial capital at taxpayer's expense? Build our own prisons, at least those who resist the Global Elite's Human 2.0. future they're creating for us. And as wild as all this is, this is really what's going on behind the scenes with governments around the world, even here in the United States.

They're financing massive amounts of money, billions of taxpayer dollars, to build the seemingly innocuous "Shielding Approach" centers, "green zones" "internment camps" whatever you want to call them because that's what they are, as the CDC recommends. In fact, you can see here some would say it's to build these "camps" all over the place, including in every city in the United States.

Home » Health » CDC announces covid internment camps for every US city

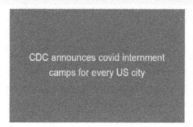

CDC announces covid internment camps for every US city

CDC announces covid internment camps for every US city

August 11, 2021   Health

Last Friday, the Governor of Tennessee signed an executive order authorizing the National Guard to medically kidnap unvaccinated people at gunpoint and forcibly take them to covid "involuntary internment" camps across the state.

PROMO CODES

Free Speech

 Fauci's Next Lockdown Victim: Free Speech

 The Dwi: Disinformation Board and the Attack on Individual Sovereignty

 Elon Musk, For the Sake of the Freedom of Speech, Buy Twitter

Free speech warning: Why she played on Indiana campus

Chapter Seven

The Signal of Human 2.0

But wait a second. How are they going to create this "next" crisis to give them the "excuse" to round up all these resisters who won't go along with the Human 2.0. vision of the future and put them into these so-called "camps?" Well let's take a look at the next section from Todd Callender in The Corona Investigative Committee interview. He clearly shares, *"It's in the frequency."*

Now that they've injected the bulk of the planet with a "computer operating system" via the Covid shots, that also acts as an antenna, they can use an "electronic signal" to do all kinds of things to people.

Viviane Fischer: *"You have the terrestrial 5G towers, and you also have the satellite things. So, what is the difference?*

Todd Callender: *"I think it's the function of which frequency they are broadcasting on. When we talk about 5G, that is just a range of frequencies. Up to 300 GHz, may do different things at different ranges. What is really troubling about it is that these 5G cell phone towers have 300,000 Giga watts of energy, that's 3 megawatts, that is enough to run a small city of 60,000 people. In each and every one of these towers, they are beaming microwave energy, the same stuff you cook food with. They* *are beaming all the time. We have demonstrations of plants and animals and birds falling out of the sky from these signals as it is. These are the powerful ones,, the strong ones, because apparently at these wavelengths they don't travel very far, and they are easily obstructed.*

The ones in space, they may be called 5G, but we really don't know what frequency they are broadcasting on. The longer the wave, the further the distance the signal travels. What we do know is that there are supposed to be 28,000 of them up there. And every single part of this planet is being beamed. It is also important to know that in 1976, the US government, the Defense Intelligence Agency, already did all this work for us. They already told us what frequencies will do or will not affect the people, all the way up from ½ a hertz to affect our mentality, whether we are happy or sad, even pain levels, and all the way up to 300 megahertz.

You might have seen, Australia, where 90 megahertz actually burned the protestors. They literally cooked the protestors. The strength of the tower and the signal are really what guide where they are putting them and what they do, and we don't know what those in space are doing. In the United States there is no law on this. OSHA has some limits on how you are going to work around these things. You have to wear protective gear to turn them off. Other than that, there is no protection. In fact, when our law firm first studied this, we found out in 2018 that in many states they made it a crime for city council members to vote against the implementation of 5G. There are no standards whatsoever. They could cook us all day long, and there's not a thing we can do about it. If you look at Wuhan, 21 million people, they either ditched their cellphones or they terminated their 5G service in the month of November. So that might be a guide to us, and our experts are saying that our cell phones, our 5G phones, are targeting systems, and I think that is what the Chinese figured out. So, some ditched their phones, some died of Covid, some didn't, but that radiation poisoning will mimic almost any disease you can think of, and they can create this with electromagnetic radiation."

So, wait a second. Frequencies or "electronic signals" including the use of 5G signals really do have an effect on people? And, depending on what signal you use, you can generate different specific effects in a person's body? Are you serious? Yes. In fact, just like Todd Callender said, this is knowledge that the governments around the world have had for a long, long time. Let me demonstrate it to you with just one technology that's been around for a while called HAARP. Let's take a look at that.

History Channel Reports: *"HAARP is comprised of 180 antennas that are 72 feet tall, and when functioning together has one giant steerable antenna. Steerable because it can aim millions of watts of ELF waves into one tiny patch of the atmosphere. The amount of energy we are talking about here is 3.6 million watts. To give you an idea of what that is, the largest radio station here in America is 50,000 watts. HAARP is 72,000, 50,000-watt radio stations injecting their entire output to a spot that is about 12 miles across, by about 2 ½ miles deep and 90 miles up.*

In an area of about 300 miles from Anchorage, Alaska, the intense energy being beamed into the sky by HAARP is beaming out to the atmosphere causing weather changes. HAARP is being used for weather modification. The military has proved it. They have admitted it in their own documents. HAARP is one of several ELF wave transmitters located all over the globe.

The United States owns three of them: one in Bakona, Ak., another in Fairbanks, Ak., and one in Arecibo, Puerto Rico. Russia has one in Vasilsursk, Russia, and the European Union has one near Tromso, Norway. Working in tandem, these transmitters could potentially alter the weather anywhere in the world. Changing the jet stream course and time, triggering massive rainstorms, or droughts. Even hurricane steering will be possible by heating up the atmosphere and building up high pressure domes that could deflect or change the course of hurricanes. Dr. Agneu experienced the power of ELF waves firsthand back in the 1980's. He was hired by an energy company that located oil and gas by using the same kind of ELF waves at much lower frequencies to carry out the search. It's a process called 'earth tomography.' But during one particular incident,

Dr. Agneu believed his use of HAARP-like ELF waves accidentally triggered an earthquake."

Dr. Agneu: *"It was in the spring of 1987 we arrived in Roseburg, Oregon. We used our ELF technology to search for oil and gas. Setting up that day, we had a little different result than what we expected, because the instant we energized it there was a 4 to 4.5 on the Richter scale earthquake that occurred."*

History Channel Reports: *"There are reportedly a total of 5 ionic spheres heaters, including HAARP, in the world today. There are possibly 20 other ionic spheres heaters all over the world."*

In other words, they're everywhere. But wait a second now, we actually have beaming signal technology in different places around the world that can control the weather and even manufacture an earthquake? Yes. It's called HAARP. Even the History Channel knows about it. And it's been around for quite some time, whether you realized it or not. But one thing they left out was this same technology could "also" be used to create a type of "death ray" that could be beamed up and over the atmosphere and then back down to an intended target anywhere in the world.

And I quote, *"HAARP Technology, can create an energy that can discharge back down the radio beam and strike the earth with a lightning bolt that is 100 times greater than any lightning bolt imaginable. And it will not strike one time, but rather 30-40 times per second until there is no longer any energy to flow. And when it strikes the ground it will vaporize the ground, water, or whatever it happens to hit, like three or four Mt. Saint Helens volcanoes going off each second that the bolt is discharging."*

Now, that's not only amazing, but if you know your Bible, it sure sounds an awful lot like the kind of trickery the False Prophet is going to use to dupe people into worshiping the Antichrist during the Seven-Year

Tribulation. He'll "cause fire to come down from Heaven…in full view of men…" You know, maybe like with HAARP technology.

Revelation 13:11-13 "Then I saw another beast, coming out of the earth. He had two horns like a lamb, but he spoke like a dragon. He exercised all the authority of the first beast on his behalf and made the earth and its inhabitants worship the first beast, whose fatal wound had been healed. And he performed great and miraculous signs, even causing fire to come down from heaven to earth in full view of men."

Well, there you have it. It's got to be real, this miracle, right? No! The Bible says these tricks that the False Prophet uses to dupe people in the Seven-Year Tribulation, including causing "fire" to come down from Heaven in full view of men, is just a bunch of trickery. That's what we see here.

2 Thessalonians 2:9 "The coming of the lawless one will be in accordance with the work of satan displayed in all kinds of counterfeit miracles, signs and wonders."

And so, the Bible says these so-called miracles, even causing fire to come down from Heaven in full view of men, by the False Prophet to dupe people into worshiping the Antichrist during the Seven-Year Tribulation are counterfeits. You know, like if he were to use HAARP technology. Since most people don't know about this technology, they get duped! In fact, another interesting side-effect of the HAARP technology is that it can also send a beam down from the "atmosphere" or "heavens" that can affect the human brain.

On Demand Reports: *"Jean Manning is a journalist who stumbled into an extreme world when she started asking questions about alternative energy sources and heard the story about an early 20th century inventor named Nikola Tesla."*

Jean Manning: *"Tesla is almost a cult hero and an overlooked genius, and he has so many inventions, bases of technology that we have today.*

Tesla talked about the Tesla Shield around the planet and talked about particle beam weaponry, something called the death ray."

On Demand Reports: *"Death ray, Jean wasn't sure where all this was leading until Mr. X called again."*

Jean Manning: *"And he said the maniacs are actually going to do it up in Alaska."*

OnDemand Reports: *"Zap oncoming missiles, disrupt the global communications, and engineer the weather. And ready? There is one more. Some people believe that the technology being tested here could be used for sinister uses involving humans. Radio waves, messing around with people's brain waves."*

"The human mind is subject to being affected by radio frequency energies, and that is what this device is. You can move the moods of large populations using this kind of technology. Question is, can they? Would they? And we believe that they can, and they will. Somewhere and, at some point, all this technology merges at some level within the Pentagon, and it happens to be in Alaska, and it happens to be now."

And yet, most people have no clue about it. But as you can see, with this technology they can "move the moods of large populations." But why would they want a technology to do that? Well, not only to "control the mood" of a population, but maybe even to "manipulate the bodies and behavior" of a population.

You see, just like they admitted in that news report, HAARP Technology can also be used to project an electronic beam that will manipulate people's behavior, depending on the frequency used. For instance, at **10.80 Hz** it can cause riotous behavior. At **7.83 Hz** it can make a person feel good or give them a state of euphoria, producing an altered state of consciousness. But HAARP Technology is not the only technology that the governments around the world have known about and have used for decades to manipulate people's bodies and brains and organs. You can also do it with microwaves, cell phone technology, Wi-Fi and, wait for it, 5G technology. Go figure.

And for proof of that, the following video transcription you're about to see is from Barrie Trower, who is a former Royal Navy Microwave Weapons Expert and former Cold War captured spy debriefer for the UK Intelligence Services. Mr. Trower is now a whistle-blower who lectures around the world on the hidden dangers from microwave weapons and everyday microwave technologies, such as mobile phones and Wi-Fi. Now, in this clip, watch how long he says Governments around the world have known about these "manipulative" properties with these kinds of beaming technologies.

Barrie Trower: *"Between 1949 and 1962, everything we needed to know about microwaves was known and published. By 1962 all of the dangers, all of the hazards, everything was known. I will not say all of them. Between the superpowers and us, the brain at that time had been studied for brainwaves, and microwaves could be used to penetrate the brain and cause behavioral changes. And by 1962 with the resonance frequencies of the organs and the brain, the cyclotronic resonance frequencies, circadian resonant frequencies, a statement was made in 1962 by the governments that birth defects, all birth defects, organs, whole organisms, all cells, brain function, all emotions, all moods, could be altered, changed, and destroyed. By 1962. Microwaves, then as now, were used as stealth weapons before they became cell phones."*

Wow! What a mouthful. So, by 1962, the governments around the world knew that "certain frequency technologies" could "have an effect in the organs and brains of people" that could "cause birth defects, effect their organs, whole organisms, all cells, brain functions, all moods," and people, by these signals, could be "altered, changed or destroyed."

Sound familiar? This is what Todd Callender was talking about in that interview clip. But that's not all. Todd also mentioned how you can use these beaming technologies like 5G to not only manipulate people's bodies and brains and organs, but it can also be done via satellite technology beaming these signals from space. And wonder of wonders, guess what Elon Musk has been up to? That's right, blanketing the whole planet with satellites. Gee, I wonder why? Let's take a look at that.

Business Insider Reports: *"You are looking at 60 satellites hurtling into the sky. And over the next few decades Elon Musk is hoping to send 42,000 of these satellites to space. Fifteen times the operational satellites that are in orbit today. It's part of Starlink, an expansive constellation for Musk and Space-X that hopes to bring to the world high beam internet, promising no more buffering and nearly instantaneous internet in every corner of the world. But experts worry that it may come at a hefty cost for space exploration.*

Nearly half of the world's population does not have access to the internet, because most internet options require an extensive track of costly underground cable, leaving many rural populations offline. Satellite internet can reach those areas."

Dave Mosher, Senior Space Correspondent: *"Traditional satellite internet is provided by a large spacecraft that was launched 22,256 miles into space to orbit around earth."*

Business Insider Reports: *"That distance means that the satellite can reach places that cables can't. But since that one satellite is meant to service a lot of people, its data capability is limited, which then means connection speed, and that signal has to travel a long way creating a lot of lag. This is where Elon Musk and Space-X comes in."*

Dave Mosher: *"Starlink is a globe encircling network of internet beaming satellites that's trying to get you online no matter where you are in the world."*

Business Insider Reports: *"As of November, Space-X has launched 700 satellites into orbit, with a plan of releasing 12,000 over the next five years, half of them by 2024. Musk wants to add another 30,000 to that, coming to a total of 42,000 satellites circling earth. All of these satellites* *will be much closer, anywhere between 200 and 400 miles above the planets low earth orbit."*

Dave Mosher: *"This reduces the connection delay that is found on the traditional satellite."*

Business Insider Reports: *"But this scheme isn't without problems. Starlink satellites are bright. They reflect the sunlight and shine it back towards earth and they end up looking like bright moving stars. As cool as it may look, that comes with problems."*

Dave Mosher: *"Starlink is most visible right before dawn and right after dusk, which is at that time that astronomers are looking for near earth objects or asteroids. Objects that could hit Earth and possibly harm us."*

Business Insider Reports: *"And as more satellites go up, so does the likelihood that they will interfere with astronomers' views."*

Dave Mosher: *"If Starlink continues to be a problem for these types of sky surveys, we may not have as much notice as we want to detect the near-Earth object and prevent it from hitting earth."*

Business Insider Reports: *"But it doesn't stop with Starlink. Amazon's Kuiper project, One Web, China's Hongvan and other projects are looking to challenge Space-X by launching their own global networks of hundreds and thousands of satellites. If they all get their way with no government regulations, we could have one hundred thousand satellites above our planet within the next 10 years."*

And what would that do to people? There's no way to escape anywhere on the whole planet from this satellite beaming technology. Why are they doing this? Is it really just to provide internet services? I don't think so. But, as a side note there, if you noticed, that guy said that all these satellites up there are blocking the view for scientists to detect near-Earth objects or asteroids from slamming into the earth and trying to prevent them from happening. Which again, is another thing that's going to occur in the Seven-Year Tribulation. Apparently, this "satellite blanket" is going to pave the way for this "asteroid" to slam into the earth. They won't be able to stop it.

Revelation 8:8-9 "The second angel sounded his trumpet, and something like a huge mountain, all ablaze, was thrown into the sea. A third of the sea turned into blood, a third of the living creatures in the sea died, and a third of the ships were destroyed."

Looks like that one's going to make it through. Too bad you had all those satellites up there blocking your view. But, as you can see, it would appear that the Global Elites have all their signal beaming bases covered, so to speak. Whether its HAARP Technology or 5G Technology or even satellite technology blanketing the planet, just like Todd said, they really could send out an "electronic signal" at the "right frequency" anywhere on the planet that could "trigger" a biological effect in people to create the next global plandemic, be it Marburg or some other "electronic" manufactured crisis.

It's already here folks. First, they got the "computing system" we saw earlier that was put inside people via the Covid shots, which will also "respond" to an "external signal," and now they are blanketing the planet with the ability to beam the right signal or frequency to give biological instructions to manipulate people for their nefarious biological purposes. Apparently "the sky's the limit" with what these Global Elites can do to us with all this technology.

But come on, is it really possible? Could the ingredients in the Covid shots really respond to an "electronic signal" from one of these sources? Well, let's examine some of the other ingredients we saw were put into these vaccines, which are not really vaccines. You tell me if they don't respond to an "electronic signal."

Paul Cherukuri, Adjunct Assistant Professor of Chemistry: *"What we have designed, and we have done it very quietly, and we are now very glad to release it to the world is this idea of Teslaphoresis, which is a discovery* *we made several years ago, and we have been developing it. Teslaphoresis is, the simplest way to understand it, is self-assembly at a distance. Long distance assembly of materials. What we did was, because we are at Rice, and we had plenty of nanotubes around, so we decided to use nanotubes. What we discovered was that these nanotubes can actually stream together and form wires by themselves under this electric field."*

Carter Kittrell, Rice University Research Scientist: *"Force acting at a distance. You can have, instead of when you normally build circuits, and things like that you have to have physical contact. Now we are talking about building circuits without actually touching them. I realized that a Tesla coil could actually do this if you designed it in a way to create a very strong forcefield in front of it. So, that was the engineering aspect of it. Once I designed the machine, then all sorts of discoveries started falling out of it."*

Lindsey Bornhoeft, Graduate student at Texas A&M University: *"Teslaphoresis is one of those things. It's a project that there are so many avenues, so many things that you can do with it. Not just making conductive wires but taking it in so many different places. Not only biomedical engineering, but taking it into a different industry like exploring different conductive materials."*

Carter Kittrell: *"This also ties, just generally, into nanotechnology that self-assembly is very big. That is, if you can get things to build themselves, just like in biology, we built ourselves."*

Narrator: *"Packing humans with nanotechnology may sound like a concept from a futuristic science novel or movie, but the truth is it's not that far off, and it could be the next big cyberthreat. How so? Nanotechnology is any technological endeavor that deals with anything with the dimensions of fewer than 100 nanometers. The concept was first brought to light in the late 1950's. It wasn't until the late 1980's that technology advanced enough that allowed scientists to work in such a small field. Nanotechnology has several applications, including food, technology, fuel, batteries, environmental causes, chemical sensors, and* *even sporting goods. The medical field is one of the most exciting for nanotechnology at the moment. Though most of the developments are still in the experimental phase. With these developments comes the ever-present technological risk of hacking."*

Nanotech in Humans: *"Building new muscle with carbon nanotubes is one such possibility. Scientists at IBM are also working on using nanotechnology to analyze DNA in a minute instead of weeks to treat cancer patients with a customized treatment plan. We are also seeing the use of nanotech in human therapy or vaccines to target specific type cells in the body or experimental nano-sponges are being tested to absorb toxins in the body. Nanotech is also being explored as an early diagnostic tool to detect cancer and infectious diseases long before our current technology is available. Some ideas include a tiny device that gets injected into the body to sensor or a medical delivery device. This all sounds positive, but there is a downside too. Is it secure? The tiny nanodevices are typically controlled by a traditional electronic device like a computer or a smart phone or server, meaning they could be very hackable.*

Some digital security experts warn, a single nanoparticle in the body with its own processor could be hacked. They also say that if a person had more than one nanoparticle in the body, which many treatments could require, the hacker could theoretically turn them into a network in the body leaving the body's own system to communicate and do their bidding. One of the most obvious and dangerous applications of biomedical hacking is ransomware. If the hacker took over your inner nanotechnology devices, they could demand a ransom with fatal consequences. If you are unwilling or unable to pay, they could easily turn your body against you and at the very least make you suffer or get sick, if not kill you. It may also be possible for an unsavory character to use nanotechnology itself against their enemies, not only in hacking attacks, such as inhalable powders to treat lungs. Some worry that nanotechnology could be an easily weaponized delivery method for bio terrorizing efforts beyond the hacking danger. Getting infected with something could be as simple as breathing the air, taking a shower, or getting a regular vaccination from your doctor."

Whoa, there it is again. I can get this nanotechnology inside of me that can then be hacked and influenced by an outside signal, from a vaccine, from a doctor. They wouldn't do that would they? They already did. And I quote, *"A tiny device gets injected into the body as a sensor or medical delivery device,"* and these *"tiny nano devices are typically controlled by a program on a traditional electronic device, like a computer, smart phone,"* (you know 5G) *"or a server, meaning they can be very hackable."*

In other words, you can be biologically manipulated now that you have this in your body. And then outside entities can, "use the body's own system to communicate and do their bidding" and it can become "an easily weaponized delivery method for bio-terrorism efforts." It's called Bio Medical Hacking. That's their term not mine, I'm not making it up. But it's real and a genuine concern, let alone a real possibility, as crazy and science fiction as it all sounds.

So, it would appear to me that this same technology that's in the vaccines really can be hacked into by some outside source, to manipulate a person's body with an "electronic signal" of sorts. You just saw the science videos and remember we're supposed to trust the science. But that's not the only vaccine ingredient that can be manipulated by an "electronic signal." So can Graphene Oxide.

Narrator: *"Humans are steadily becoming bionic. That's not the latest Sci-Fi movie we are describing. It's a very probably and very close future thanks to the wonderful material called Graphene. One of the things that makes Graphene so cool is that it is the thinnest material you can imagine. It's just one atom thick. That means this material is mathematically two-dimensional, and you can hold this single layer of atoms in your hands. Doesn't that blow your mind? Surprisingly, Graphene isn't a unique or rare substance. In fact, it has the same carbon structure as the graphite you use every day when you draw or write with your pencil!*

At the same time in 0.03 inches of graphite equals 3 million Graphene layers! Dr. Konstantin Novoselov and Professor Andre Geim discovered the wonder material in 2004 at the University of Manchester. They were examining how efficient graphite is as a transistor. The story goes that Graphene appeared thanks to sticky tape. After they stuck this tape to a piece of graphite and pulled free a single layer of the material. This left them with Graphene. In 2010 they were awarded a Nobel Prize for their invention.

Graphene is incredibly stretchy. It can stretch as much as 25 percent of its length. This material is also really stiff. It's the hardest material people know about – even harder than diamonds, and that says a lot. In fact, nothing less than an elephant balancing on a sharpened pencil will be able to pierce Graphene. Despite being two-dimensional, Graphene can still be seen. This single layer of atoms is perfectly visible to the naked eye, and you don't even have to bother with a microscope.

One more great thing about Graphene is its relationship with electricity. This material carries electricity more quickly, more precisely, and more efficiently than any other known material. The reason is that the current density of Graphene is many million times better than that of copper. As for its intrinsic mobility, it's much better than silicon. But electrons have no resistance when they move through Graphene. As a result, people can potentially use Graphene to produce batteries that will have 10 times the electrical retention capacity of anything we have today.

One more quality of Graphene that scientists find extremely interesting is that it expands when cool and shrinks when it gets warm. There are no other examples of materials with a similar quality. All normal substances act in the opposite way. They become larger when they are heated and smaller when they get cold. That is probably why the E.U. devoted $1.3 billion to research that's supposed to last for a decade. (from 2013 to 2023). This research is intended to find out how Graphene can alter the very principles of the electronics, health, construction, and energy sectors.

How can Graphene be used?

There are countless opportunities that Graphene can provide humanity.

151

Scientists at the University of Illinois have determined that Graphene can assist in detecting cancerous cells in the body. Researchers from the University of Texas have invented temporary tattoos that are based on Graphene. These tattoos are far from a simple body decoration. They can keep track of a person's vitals, including their level of hydration and skin temperature."

"Watch as this assembly line pumps out tiny machines called micromotors. These micromotors are only a few hundred micrometers long and they can move when put in a magnetic field. Scientists propose that micromotors like these could one day deliver drugs inside the body. Micromotors can propel themselves in a number of ways. The popular way to get around is to use a chemical fuel, such as hydrogen peroxide. Materials in the motors react with the fuel to produce jets of gas bubbles that push the tiny particles forward. But this approach can introduce unwanted toxic compounds into the motor's surroundings. Ditching the fuel and just using an external magnetic field to move the motors avoids those toxicity issues.

It's a strategy that's also well-suited for biomedical applications, because magnetic fields can penetrate the body. Now, a team of researchers at the Chinese University of Hong Kong and Huazhong University of Science and Technology have developed novel magnetic-responsive micromotors made of Graphene. Researchers can easily attach other molecules to Graphene."

Gregory Snyder: "I work in the team of K Becker, and I work on designing graphene nanopores to sequence DNA at the single molecule level. The idea of DNA sequencing is to read the content of your genome. And what you want is a recorder that can read the sequence of your DNA and for that you need a recorder that is not bigger than the size of the single base. So, we are using graphene, because graphene is only one of the things that could be used by a physician in his office to sequence the DNA of one of his patients in only a few minutes rather than few days.

Graphene oxide is placed next to a cell phone. When the phone is turned on the graphene oxide starts reacting to EMF's. Sending a call causes the clump of graphene to start moving and growing. It is squirming all around, but when the phone call is ended, it is completely still. The phone is held over the graphene oxide, but it doesn't affect it at all. They turn the phone on again and "It's alive!" 5G anyone?

"Wonder material graphene connects to a 5G network, coffee machines and self-driving cars. For about ten years, graphene has been the key technology for taking electronic devices into the new era. A scientific article published in Nature Reviews Materials analyzes the possibilities of using graphene in the future world of 'the internet of things.' Graphene is a one atom thick carbon material. Within the big international 10-year graphene project, Estonians are promoting the activities of the health and environment package."

Narrator: *"This transparent strip is made of one of the strongest materials on earth, and now we are going to inject this into your body. Could it make your cells regenerate faster? Does graphene ever leave your body? Does the vaccine contain graphene? Here's what would happen if you were injected with graphene.*

This material first seen in 2004 is only one atom thick. Found after peeling off transparent tape from graphite, the minerals stuck to the tape was named graphene, and it might be the first two-dimensional substance ever discovered. But don't be fooled by its size. Graphene is 100 times stronger than steel and powerful enough to repel most gases and liquids.

Discovering it has revolutionized battery and information technology, but if these graphene atoms entered your bloodstream, what would happen to your cells? You can create graphene oxide by oxidizing graphite. And this nanoparticle, graphene oxide, can be used in medical treatments since it breaks down in water fast. Drugs injected into your system could be delivered to their destination thanks to this cheap and readily available substance. Studies in lab rats have shown that graphene has caused tumors to shrink. Other tests show that graphene might even make your bones regenerate quicker. But all this comes at a cost. While graphene has quickly revolutionized the tech and medical industries, we still don't know what this mineral can do to us in the long run."

Except for the Global Elites. They have a plan for it. But it looks to me like Graphene Oxide is not only currently being used in the medical community, all over the place, including in the vaccine industry, but it really can be manipulated by an "electronic signal," including 5G for various biological effects. I wonder what they'll do with that.

Wait a second, wait a second! The media and so-called medical experts have been vehemently denying the fact that they put these nano materials into their vaccines, which can respond to an "electronic signal." They've denied it until they're blue in the face. Well, just because they "deny it," doesn't make it true. How many times do we have to be lied to by these so-called media and medical experts before we wake up? The fact is, the media outlets, the whole medical community, and the Global Elites have literally lied throughout this whole pandemic phase, time, and time again; and yet I'm supposed to believe and trust what they have to say on anything, let alone the true ingredients in the vaccine and their 5G manipulative technology? No way!

In fact, let me give you just a quick, easy example of how many times we've been lied to by these Global entities. The following list are the things that were labeled as "myths" and "misinformation," but of course were later proven to be true.

- We said, "The asymptomatic vaccinated are spreading the virus equally as with unvaccinated symptomatic infected." They denied it but it turned out to be true.
- We said, "The vaccines cannot protect adequately against new variants, such as Delta and Omicron." They denied it but it turned out to be true.
- We said, "Natural immunity is far superior to vaccine immunity and is most likely lifelong." They denied it but it turned out to be true.

- We said, "Vaccine immunity not only wanes after several months, but all immune cells are impaired for prolonged periods, putting the vaccinated at a high risk of all infections and cancer." They denied it but it turned out to be true.
- We said, "COVID vaccines can cause a significant incidence of blood clots and other serious side effects." They denied it but it turned out to be true.
- We said, "The vaccine proponents will demand numerous boosters as each variant appears on the scene." They denied it but it turned out to be true.
- We said, "Fauci will insist on the Covid vaccine for small children and even babies." They denied it but it turned out to be true.
- We said, "Vaccine passports will be required to enter a business, fly in a plane, and use public transportation." They denied it but it turned out to be true.
- We said, "There will be internment camps for the unvaccinated (as in Australia, Austria, and Canada)" They denied it, but it turned out to be true.
- We said, "The unvaccinated will be denied employment." They denied it but it turned out to be true.
- We said, "There are secret agreements between the government, elitist institutions, and vaccine makers." They denied it but it turned out to be true.
- We said, "Many hospitals were either empty or had low occupancy during the pandemic." They denied it but it turned out to be true.
- We said, "The spike protein from the vaccine enters the nucleus of the cell, altering cell DNA repair function." They denied it but it turned out to be true.
- We said, "Hundreds of thousands have been killed by the vaccines and many times more have been permanently damaged." They denied it but it turned out to be true.
- We said, "Early treatment could have saved the lives of most of the 700,000 who died." They denied it but it turned out to be true.

- We said, "Vaccine-induced myocarditis (which was denied initially) is a significant problem and clears over a short period." They denied it but it turned out to be true.
- We said, "Special deadly lots (batches) of these vaccines are mixed with the mass of other Covid-19 vaccines." They denied it but it turned out to be true.

Can you say, "Liar, liar pants on fire!?" And I'm supposed to trust these guys when they say there's no substances in these Covid shots that could potentially respond to an "electronic signal" that could then manipulate the human body for who knows what purposes, at least for those that got the Covid shots? I don't think so! I'll never trust these guys!

Besides, not so surprisingly, some brave doctors are now coming out, risking it all, including their lives, by blowing the whistle on the fact that these Global Elites and the whole medical community know very well that these vaccines, which are not vaccines, do contain materials that will respond to an "electronic signal."

Stew Peters: *"First I want to start off with this breaking news. Scientists have delivered, exclusively to you, evidence, proof of nanotechnology inside these bioweapon shots."*

Maria Zeee: *"Yes, as you know, Australia is under extreme medical tyranny. Medical experts there don't speak up. It is very rare. So, they contacted me. They wanted me to bring this information out. They had been researching it for some time. They told me that they had not been able to sleep. Now what they have found in these vaccines, they aren't vaccines, I don't want to call them that anymore, undeniably graphene oxide. What they presented to me may actually be the reason why people now have vaccine injuries, auto-immune deficiency syndrome. They say they have a lot more for me. This was specifically Pfizer at this point, but they have shown what's happening in the blood as well and they have more coming for me. They have got to be very careful; I'm obviously protecting their identity at all costs. It's shocking. It just confirms what other experts around the world are finding under the microscope.*

All images may look different, but they are all the same, it's graphene oxide. It is nanotechnology inside the people in order to change what it means to be human. I mean these people want us to be walking cyborgs for goodness sakes."

Stew Peters: *"Yes, they do. They want us to be anything but the image of God which is how we were created in His likeness."*

Maria Zeee: *"I also had Sen. Malcolm Roberts on the show. He is also saying this stuff. He has a group that has gone from start to finish. They recorded the whole thing. When they go to the frig, open the vial, put it under the microscope and he has witnessed it in front of his eyes."*

Dr. Buttar: *"Essentially what appears to be coming down the pipeline is that what has been introduced within the vaccine, regardless of the type, they have introduced into individuals, through these vaccines and the subsequent boosters, other components. We have all heard of some of these components. They talk about the nanotechnology, there's of course the spike protein, all these different things that have been found. There's been the graphene oxide, all sorts of different things that have been found within these vaccines and still the thing that we haven't discovered, I know, about a year ago they found Round Up, that's a weed killer, in the vaccines. What is Round Up, a weed killer doing inside of a vaccine? We don't understand that.*

Obviously, there are all sorts of things that are being found that shouldn't be in the vaccines. But this portion that I'm going to talk about now is something that has been, I guess the right word would be, I had suspicions that they were introducing something into the vaccine that are designed to cause a detrimental effect at a time when they want that detrimental effect to take place. Meaning that it is almost like a sleeper-cell within your own body. It's there, you don't know it's there, there's no effect from it but it can be called upon or triggered based upon any type of signal or chemical or maybe two inert relatively innocuous ingredients so that when they come together, they cause something to happen. And that would be the trigger, if you will, that would cause these sleeper cells in your body to awaken.

Now, I felt that for a long time, in fact, even before Covid that they would be introducing something into our body that shouldn't be there. But now we have confirmation of this, and I'm just going to specifically talk to you about what is actually in there. Essentially, from two different sources, we have confirmation, and I have talked to one of those sources myself. There is something within the vaccine that is being considered a bioweapon, and again is not a new term. But this particular component within the vaccine is almost like a payload. Now a payload is where there is a detonation, you have a truck or a trailer that has a bunch of dynamite or explosives. They call it a payload. It is designed to deliver a massive eruption or detonation. They call it a payload because it wouldn't be like a normal onslaught. It would be more like a massive onslaught. So, there's going to be a payload with some type of pathogen that will be activated by a sequence of 5G bursts, and these will be basically of a 16 to 18 GHz frequency, and they will be essentially three bursts that will be sequential and last a minute. Those will be designed so that these bursts will create a signal that will release this payload that is within this hydrogel component of the vaccine.

So, what exactly is in there? There is supposed to be three pathogens and these three pathogens, I'm not exactly sure what these pathogens are, but one of them is what they call the Marburg virus which is essentially a pathogen that mimics the hemorrhagic fever. A component similar to that. And according to, and you can look it up, it says there is a 22 percent up to a 90 percent mortality rate, and Google says it's an 88 percent mortality. Meaning that for every 100 people who get it, 88 out of 100 will die. Now, that's designed to justify, that once that release has taken place, that signal from the 5G Tower, the three bursts that last one minute each and it's the 18 GHz frequency, it will cause the hydrogel to release this payload of the virus or the viral load. There are supposed to be three different types, and one of them is the Marburg virus.

When that happens, everybody that had the vaccine, and these boosters will have this Marburg virus released and again we know that it's a 22 up to 90 percent mortality rate. But we know that is when somebody empowers it in a natural way, if you will. When it's inside of your body already and released inside your body, it's probably going to be a 100 percent mortality rate. Meaning, everybody that has it, it's going to be triggered and it's going to be released. When that happens, it's obvious these people are going to die, not hundreds of thousands, but millions and millions of people worldwide, they are going to have this effect. The most grievous thing is that those massive numbers of deaths will then cause a sequence of events to start and once these cells burst and release the Marburg epidemic then the Center for Disease Control and The World Health Organization will assume control, because there are a massive number of deaths taking place."

Boy, have we been lied to! And again, this is what these brave doctors, as you just saw, and legal experts like Todd Callender are saying. This technology that is now inside of people who took the Covid shots, will give these Global

Elites the ability to "trigger" them with an "electronic signal" to create the next plandemic. One even bigger than the last one, that they really have planned for us to create the excuse to grab even more power and total control across the whole planet. This is sick.

And just like Todd Callender said, the "trigger" event might very well include the creation or release of the Marburg Virus inside of those who got the Covid shots. Which by the way, for those of you who don't know what the Marburg Virus is, they are not only prepping us that it could oddly enough be the next "plandemic" go figure, but how did they know that?

I quote, *"Marburg is one of the deadliest viruses we know of, killing as many as 9 out of 10 people it infects. It begins with a fever, severe headache, and muscle pains. This is often followed by watery diarrhea, stomach pain, nausea, and vomiting, accompanied by extreme exhaustion and lethargy."*

"Many people go on to develop severe viral hemorrhagic fever and in severe cases have blood in their vomit and feces and may bleed from their nose, gums, and sexual organs. The onslaught of the virus is so extreme that most people die 8-9 days after infection."

And there's no cure as this guy shares. What is the Marburg Virus?

Mortality Rate: *"The percentage of people likely to die out of everyone who contracts the disease. It varies widely from one illness to another. To give you a rough idea, Covid 19 has mortality rate of 1.4%, typhoid 15%, tuberculosis 43%. Marburg virus is so deadly that during the worst outbreak it kills 90% of those infected. That's a massive rate of fatality. It's an untreatable virus, so once you've got it, there's no cure. One slip up when treating a patient, disposing of their possessions, or conducting an autopsy, and your odds of survival are one in ten. And it's not a nice way to go either.*

Symptoms: *The first signs you've been infected with Marburg are pretty common to most illnesses. Fever, headache, sore joints, rashes. Next comes diarrhea which can last a week. On the third day you can expect to start vomiting with the accompanying abdominal pain and cramps. The diarrhea and vomiting are especially unfortunate as Marburg spreads through bodily fluids. Anyone caring for you in this stage of the illness has* *a high likelihood of contracting it too, unless they wrap themselves in multiple layers of PPE and dose everything in chlorine.*

Finally, after worsening for a few days, the internal hemorrhaging begins. You start bleeding from every orifice, and at this point you're beyond saving. Previous patients have bled from their eyes, nose, gums, and needle puncture points. Hemorrhaging can even be seen beneath the skin. Most people die of excessive blood loss. And die eight to nine days after the first symptoms begin.

Treatment: *It's known as the untreatable disease for a reason. Once you're infected, there's nothing that can be done. Doctors will provide you with pain relief to ease suffering. But there's no cure."*

Well, that's encouraging. No wonder they picked it. So, could this Marburg virus really be what the Global Elites will "trigger" inside those who got the Covid shots with an "electronic signal?" Well, it would appear that way, because as Todd Callender said, "If they weren't planning on this, then why did they launch The Marburg Prep Act back in late 2020." As you can see here.

So, whether an "electronic signal" goes out from these Global Elites that creates Marburg in those who got the Covid shots, or something else they decide to "trigger" inside of people to create the next Global Plandemic, it really does appear that this is a viable conclusion based on the evidence. Be a Berean, don't stick your head in the sand. In fact, maybe the next "triggered Plandemic" will be what we're also hearing in the news. Could the next Plandemic be the Monkeypox Virus, as seen here?

DW.com News Reports: *"Now, authorities in the U.S. state of Massachusetts have recorded their first case of the rare monkeypox virus. Several European countries have reported cases, most recently in France. U.S. doctors are now investigating whether the Massachusetts case is related to the European outbreaks."*

Myles Tweedie: *"Monkeypox is a rare viral infection usually found in small mammals in Central Africa. The spread of the virus is usually caused by people traveling to those areas. That's why doctors at the Massachusetts General Hospital in the U.S. were initially surprised to be confronted with the disease in a patient."*

Erica Shenoy, Infection Control Unit: *"During the course of their admission, they were identified as a possible monkeypox suspect. And this was really unusual, because the patient had no travel history, no exposure to animals that would be known to be reservoirs."*

Myles Tweedie: *"Doctors are now working to establish whether the infection is connected to small outbreaks currently being seen in Europe. Italy and Sweden have become the latest countries to confirm cases; following Britain, Portugal, and Spain."*

Yeah, and just how did that get started, especially when people haven't traveled to Africa and weren't even around the animals that typically carry it? Go figure, they are starting to say maybe this will be the next plandemic unleashed upon us.

Or should I say unleashed "inside" those who got the Covid shots. And I say that because guess what else just happens to be inside those Covid shots? Not just Marburg, Ebola, and others, but Monkey parts! I kid you not! This is straight from the FDA gov's website.

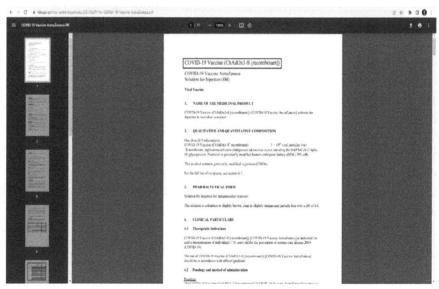

And as you can see, the ingredients in the Covid vaccine clearly say it contains, **"Replication-defective vector based on a chimpanzee adenovirus."**

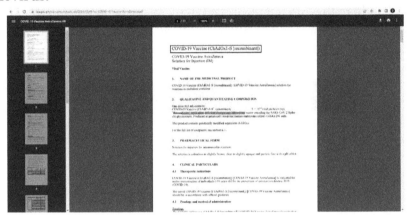

Now, why would you put monkey parts in the vaccines on top of the Marburg and Ebola and the other dangerous infections stuff we saw were in there earlier? Well, maybe this gives the Global Elites options when their "trigger signal" goes out. Will it be Ebola, Marburg, Monkeypox, or all three, or something else? Who knows? All of them or any of them will do the trick! And if you think they're being honest about this latest Monkeypox virus, think again! As you can see here, they held a global pandemic simulation on Monkeypox, in advance, just like they did with the Covid-19 Plandemic. Again, get our previous documentary *"The*

Great Covid Deception," where we lay out that pre-planned evidence as well.

But here they go again. In fact, they're not only getting the media to go in on this preplanned Monkeypox Virus agenda, but they even outlined last year how they are going to phase it in on us!

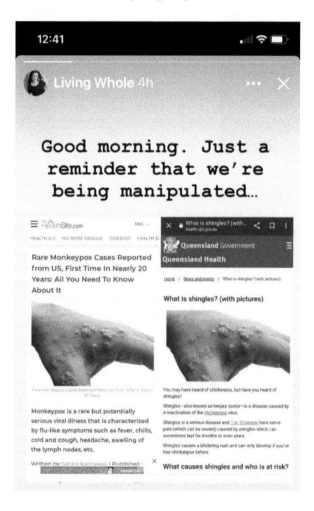

Monkeypox Was a Table-Top Simulation Only Last Year

BY MICHAEL SENGER MAY 20, 2022 3 MINUTE READ

SHARE | PRINT | EMAIL

As you can see here in their simulation plan, they have plans to release Monkeypox this year. And then at the beginning of the following year, it's going to be in multiple countries, causing supposed millions of deaths.

Figure 1. Scenario Design Summary

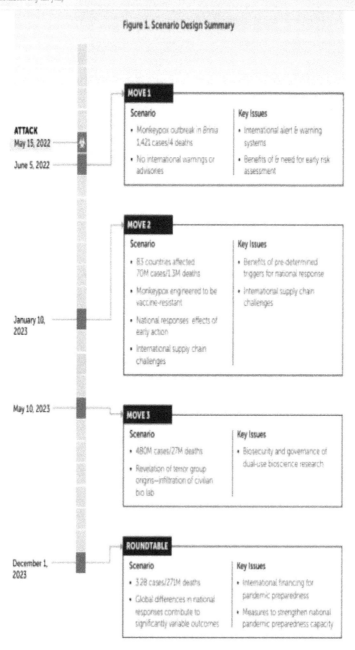

And I'm sure they'll have to step in and grab even more control, and take away even more of our freedoms and rights, you know, like they did with the preplanned Covid-19 agenda. But I wonder how they're going to start all of this, all of a sudden, all over the world? Can you say, "Trigger the event with an electronic signal." As crazy as that sounds, the evidence seems to be pointing in that very direction.

Chapter Eight

The Super Soldiers of Human 2.0

But speaking of crazy, that's still just the tip of the iceberg of what these Global Elites could do with these "frequencies" and "electronic trigger signals" on a global basis to people's bodies, that is, to those who took the Covid shots. Now that they have this electronic operating system inside of people via the shots, this genetic manipulative operating system could not only track and monitor people across the whole planet, as well as monitor their bodies and even give them instructions to alter their genetic makeup and/or possibly trigger another plandemic inside of them; but believe it or not, they might also be used to turn some people into, wait for it, Super Soldiers.

I know it sounds totally crazy, too, but let's take a look at yet another statement made by Todd Callender in The Corona Investigative Committee Interview. Are Super Soldiers really on the horizon with all this technology the Global Elites are using on us as well? Let's take a look.

Viviane Fischer: *"Now can you explain about the vaccine shot? So, do you think this is really basically control, like getting you on the hook to survive? Is there anything that you could imagine that would be like an* *enhancement, like you would be able to intake oxygen better so you can basically live under the sea?"*

Todd Callender: *"For sure! Circa 2001, the U.S Government, the Department of Defense, made its way into the gene therapy business for exactly what it is that you are describing. Then, in 2005, they got a special exclusion from the Department of Justice as it relates to informed consent. The Department of Justice basically said, for the purposes of gene modification, the FDA is no longer involved. Health and Human Services are involved. And for purposes of informed consent that we all know comes from Nuremberg, no longer apply in the traditional sense. All you have to do is let people know that you are doing genetic therapies, that means gene modification and you don't even have to tell them. You just have to make it so they could find out. So, the U.S. military have been doing gene modification at least since 2005, for exactly what you just described. Super Soldier program, whatever, swimming under the ocean, flying, I don't know, but it already exists.*

When you do a search, if you type in North Korea Super Soldiers, you'll see Kim Jong-Un already brought his out and did a demonstration, beating these guys with sledgehammers. They seem to be puncture proof and extraordinarily durable and fast and probably require far less food. Something along those lines. So, the answer is yes, for sure."

Viviane Fischer: *"This means you can actually transform a previous normal human being, during his or her lifetime, into this sort of special forces person with special abilities. It's not for the next generation, it's immediately."*

Todd Callender: *"It's now, and, in fact, there are some signs in this study that show that they can now download information straight into their brain. There was a case that the army did years ago that just a regular old soldier, they downloaded information and he was out flying helicopters later that day. I'm a pilot and I can tell you it takes a long time to master those skills. So, that technology already exists, exactly as you described."*

Dr. Reiner Fuellmich: *"So, Moderna wasn't joking when they said we can program human beings now."*

Todd Callender: *"That's right, Charles Lieber, really the guy behind that, he's sitting in jail now. If you look back at his 2009 Harvard study, he was able to autonomically weld transistors into the lipid nanoparticles. He could control them. He could program them and move around and be autonomous; and he turned the lipid nanoparticles into nanobots. And with those nanobots they are able to actually do exactly what you describe. They crawl around in the brain. They can receive information. They can deliver a payload to one particular part of the body. But he was the man that made all of that possible, along with Dr. Craig Venter who created synthetic life. He was the guy who sequenced the human genome; and he was able, about three years ago, to sever some heads on some pigs, wait three days, and then reanimate the pigs without the heads. They did a study with ferrets relating to coronavirus. They found that they had killed the ferrets and buried them, and the ferrets came back and dug themselves out. So, there is this extra component also of immortality if you can imagine that. I have the articles on that."*

Viviane Fischer: *"That is very creepy. Can you elaborate on what it's like, biological graphene? What is the point of having this in your body? Is it really just to kill you off like the 5G thing?"*

Todd Callender: *"No, there's three things. Number one, it's extraordinarily conductive. So, if a person with graphene oxide receives a signal, if I understand it again from our experts, they will be able to produce a 1 terahertz signal. They become a battery, and Bill Gates actually has a patent on this, a human battery. So, number one, they become generators, electricity generators.*

Number two, they become sources of intelligence. Everything that person sees, hears, and does; it's connected to the bio-net of things and every other such person and cell phone tower and, in fact, the Cloud. They all become bio machines. They are capable of detecting everything, sight, sound, touch, feel, taste, all of that. On top of that, graphene is the single most durable and strong substance on this planet. So, when you see Kim Jong-Un's super soldiers getting hit with hammers in the head to no avail, that's why. You can't even puncture graphene's single molecular layer.

Lastly, it is self-assembling. So, when you add Teslaphoresis, when you add electrical current graphene oxide or graphene hydroxide, it naturally self-assembles and turns into a conductive circuit. So, you are getting all the things out of the benefit of graphene. There's multiple uses of course. And then I think to your point you will have people they don't want to use it, and they will just turn it off. It's gone."

Wow! Like a kill switch. Is this sick or what? But where do you even start with this? What a mouthful here! First of all, did you catch that one part where Todd said some of the plans with this genetic operating system inside of people, is to create a "human battery," and there's actual patents on that? Is it just me, or does that sound like this Hollywood movie scene? Remember this in the Matrix movie?

The scene opens with Keanu Reeves sitting in the chair, just getting hooked up for the treatment. A woman, possibly the assistant, is locking down his feet while Laurence Fishburne is pushing his head down into position. He tells him that it will feel a little weird. Suddenly there is an electrical shock that goes into his head, and he screams in pain. Then just as suddenly, he is somewhere else. In a white room looking around. He turns around in this empty room and then a man appears. The man tells him, "This is the construct. It's our loading program. We can load anything from clothing, equipment, weapons, training simulations, anything we need." As he gets closer, he realizes it is Laurence Fishburne.

He asks this man, *"So, right now we are inside a computer program?"* The answer is, *"Is it so hard to believe? Your clothes are different. The plugs in your arms and head are gone. Your hair has changed. Your appearance now is what we call residual self-imaging. It's the mental projection of your digital self. What is real? How do you define real? If you are talking about what you can feel, what you can smell and taste and see, real is just electrical signals interpreted by your brain. This is the*

world that you know. The world as it was at the end of the 20ᵗʰ century."
He turns on a TV so that Reeves can see what he is talking about. *"This is now just a neural interactive simulation that we call the Matrix."*

"You have been living in a dream world. This is the world as it exists today." Again, on the TV screen a futurist scene is shown, but as they sit there it becomes the reality of where they are sitting. He continues, *"Welcome to the desert of the Real. We have only bits and pieces of information, but what we know for certain is that at some point in the early part of the 21ˢᵗ century all of mankind was united in celebration. We marveled at our own magnificence we gave birth to AI, a singular consciousness that spawned an entire race. We don't know who struck first, us or them, but we know that it was us that scorched the sky. At the time they were dependent on solar power, and it was believed that they would be unable to survive without any energy sources. Throughout human history, we have been dependent on machines to survive. Fate, it seems, is not without a sense of irony. The human body generates more bioelectricity than a 120-volt battery and over 25,000 BTUs in body heat.*

Combined with a form of fusion, the machines had found all the energy they would ever need. There are fields, endless fields, where human beings are no longer born. We are grown. For the longest time I wouldn't believe it. Then I saw the fields with my own eyes. Watched them liquefy the dead, so they could be fed intravenously. Standing there facing the purely horrifying procedure, I came to the obviousness of the truth. What is the Matrix? Control. The Matrix is a computer-generated dreamworld, built to keep us under control in order to change human beings into batteries."

And according to Todd Callender, Bill Gates even has a patent on it. But you might be thinking, "Come on. Surely, that's not part of what the Global Elites are planning on doing to us, making us into "human batteries" for some nefarious purpose?" Well, speaking of Hollywood, I believe Hollywood is being used and has been used for many years to slowly but surely prepare us for the Matrix-type reality that these Global Elites are building for us, including the use of AI or Artificial Intelligence, to get the job done, just like in that movie premise. And as sick and gross as that is, it's not just turning us into "human batteries" either, but believe it or not, it could turn us into Super Soldiers.

Let's go back to what else Todd said in the last interview clip. He said apparently another plan these Global Elites have, with all this genetic manipulation technology inside of people who took the Covid shots, is to make them, at least some of them, into real life Super Soldiers. Again, just like in Hollywood movies we've been seeing in the last several years. Go figure.

But is this legit? Well again, let's remind ourselves of what the propaganda machine, also known as Hollywood, has been preparing us for many years now. Not just a Matrix-type reality, but even the existence of Genetically modified Super Soldiers. Let's take a look at this propaganda.

Clip from Universal Soldier

"It was a top-secret government project, designed to create the perfect soldier. Cryogenically preserved and genetically enhanced, programmed to obey."

Soldier: *"Pack them in ice, all of them!"*

"No man would ever again have to die for the service of his country."

"We are at the tower. Okay, here we go. Who are these guys?" Guns are pointed at a man that is running down the side of the dam.

Reporter: *"30 hostages are being held inside the base of the structure."*

As the reporter is telling the TV audience what is going on, there is shooting going on outside.

They were sending their Universal Soldiers to rescue the hostages but there was one thing they didn't count on.

"At the end of the mission he became completely unresponsive."

Inside the machine is a man.

"Do you really think I would allow the regeneration of dead soldiers?"

As the reporter starts to investigate what is going on you hear the one in charge saying, *"Stop the girl. Shoot her if you have to."*

It takes one memory to awaken him. The reporter asks him, *"What did they do to you?"* He replies, *"I don't know. But I'd like to find out."*

One can't be controlled. The other cannot be stopped.

"This mission has been canceled!" But the one that can't be stopped says, *"I'm giving the orders from now on. I'm going to teach them all."* As the soldier is fighting the bad soldier by racing in buses, the bad soldier calls out to the good one, *"Are we having fun yet?"*

The ultimate weapons of danger have declared war on each other.

A clip from X-Men

The World is Changing

"We are seeing the beginning of another stage of human evolution."

"The truth is that mutants are very real, and they are among us."

Man is Evolving

"We must know who they are, and, above all, what they can do."

The time is coming when all that we are afraid will be all that can save us.

"Who are you people, what kind of place is this?"

"I'm Professor Charles Xavier, I built this school where mutants can learn to focus their powers in a positive way and also learn that mankind is not evil. Just uninformed."

"You will be safe here. There is a war brewing between the mutants and humanity."

"There is a war coming, are you on the right side?"

Trust a few, Wolverine, Cyclops, Storm, Rogue, Jean Grey, Professor X, and fear the rest, Sabretooth, Mystique, Toad, Magneto.

"I've never seen anything like this before."

"We are the future Charles, not them. They no longer matter."

A clip from Captain America

As the guys are waiting for their names to be called for their physical for the draft, they are reading the paper about the deaths occurring by the Nazis.

"Boy there are a lot of deaths going on over there. Kind of makes you think twice about enlisting."

His name is called, and he proceeds to go in for his check-up. When he gets to the counter he is asked:

"What did your dad die of?" He answers, *"Mustard gas. He was in the 107th infantry. I was hoping I could be assigned..."* Another question, *"Mother?"* He answers, *"She was a nurse in the TB ward."* The guy behind the counter says, *"Sorry, son!"* But the recruit says, *"Just give me a chance."* The guy behind the counter says, *"You would be denied just for your asthma alone."* Again, he tries, *"Isn't there anything you can do?"*

The next scene is where he is in the machine getting ready to be injected with something to make him stronger.

Professor: *"Ladies and Gentlemen, we begin with these micro injections into the subject's major muscles. The infusion will cause immediate cellular change, and then we will stimulate growth. The subject will be saturated with vitamins."*

Steve Rogers: *"That wasn't so bad."* After he received the first shot.

Professor: *"That was penicillin."* *"Gentlemen, fusion. Beginning in 5, 4, 3, 2, 1."* And all the containers start to unload and run down the tubes into Steve Rogers' body. The lever is pulled, and Steve is hoisted up in this cylinder for the drugs to begin their work. He is completely encased in this cylinder.

The final connection is hooked to the cylinder and the work begins. Everyone is watching with bated breath to see what the results of this will be, if he even lives through it.

The Professor knocks on the window to see if he is all right. He answers back, *"It's probably too late to go to the bathroom, right?"*

Professor: *"We will proceed."* Buttons are pushed, wheels are turned, the gauge is being watched as it climbs up to 100 percent. Meanwhile, Steve Rogers is screaming in pain. One of the ladies in the crowd watching starts yelling at the professor to shut it down. They run to the panel to start shutting it down, but a voice is coming from the cylinder saying, *"NO! I can do this."* When it reaches maximum power, sparks start flying, and it slowly shuts down. Everyone watches with caution. Is he still alive? They open the cylinder, and a brand-new man is standing in there, totally rebuilt. He is muscle-bound, ready to take on the world. He is Captain America. He is asked, *"How do you feel?"* He answers, *"It's over."*

The next scene is Captain America working on the street, saving the world. He chased a car a speed faster than the car. Since he is still rather new at this, he loses his balance and falls through a store window. The next thing that he finds out he can do is jump from car to car driving down the street. The bad guy jumps into a submarine, and Captain America is also able to swim like a fish. He opens up the top of the submarine and pulls out the guy and throws him out of the water onto the pier. As he is standing over the guy, he looks at his arms and is amazed at how strong he is. He is a whole new man.

Good thing that was just a movie. Nope. It's propaganda. This is the next reality that these Global Elites are preparing us for with all this genetic manipulation technology. As they say, "It's the next step in human evolution," whether you want it or not. And it's not just being promoted via Hollywood for these Global Elites, it's already well underway! What else did Todd say? It's already being done in North Korea. They're already parading their Super Soldiers around.

Is that true? Well, let's be a Berean and take a look at a transcript of this video footage and you tell me if Todd once again knew what he was talking about.

WION Reports: *"Now, let's tell you what is happening in North Korea. But before we play out the story for you, here's a bit of advice. Don't try any of this at home or outside for that matter. Don't try it. North Korea, we know, is a country that makes headlines for bizarre or dangerous developments, a country where one man rules twenty-five million people. His whims are the law. He makes his subjects do irrational things. Watch. Let the pictures do the talking."*

A crowd of spectators, sitting in rows of chairs, are watching two men fight on the pavement in front of them. The men are dressed in military-type uniforms. They kick and punch each other. One man knocks the other out, then bends his arm.

Next scene: Pairs of men are holding what look like cinder blocks at shoulder height. Other men run one at a time, jump and kick the block shattering it. Runners kick, twist, and kick other blocks. All the blocks shatter when they are kicked. Then the crowd cheers.

Piles of what look like roof tiles are stacked three or more high on about two-foot-high metal supports. There is a row of many of these. By each pile, a man is kneeling on one knee. The kneeling man has his hand on the pile of tiles. A different man with a sledgehammer, crashes it down on the hand, breaking the brick tiles beneath it. They do this one at a time going down the row.

Then men hit other men with what looks like two-by-fours. These are all military exercises to show how tough the men are and that they can endure almost anything. A self-defense exhibition. More clapping and cheering from the spectators.

There's a low board, maybe two feet square, with nails sticking point up. A man takes two glass bottles, breaks them, gathers the broken glass onto a cloth, and lays back down on the glass. Another places a cement block on his chest and splits it by hitting it with a sledgehammer. The man that was laying down jumps up. The crowd claps and cheers.

WION Reports: *"You see that? There's more. Men break two layers of bricks. One man runs and smashes his head on them. Others have rocks smashed on their body, followed by some hammering on their hands. And one-man smashes two glass bottles together, adds them to a pile of shard, and lies on them, shirtless. All of this while the supreme leader sits and grins with his ministers. This was not an episode of North Korea's Got Talent. This was Kim Jong-Un telling the world to not mess with his country.*

The footage we showed you was aired on the North Korean state media. They say it was a message for their enemies. North Korean soldiers have quote, unquote 'iron fists' to protect their country. I'm sure they do. But the level of self-harm they inflicted here makes me wonder if North Korea needs enemies at all. Also, who exactly are these people, are they super soldiers? That's what social media is calling them. They're certainly extraordinary, enhanced soldiers, they have been genetically engineered."

Yeah, looks that way to me. And North Korea is not the only one. It's now public knowledge that China is openly admitting to doing the exact same thing as well with their soldiers.

MSNBC Reports: *"So, it sounds like something out of a movie. The threat of a bunch of human weapons with biologically enhanced capabilities. Pretty sure that's the plotline of Captain American. But the reality, we might be talking about is Captain China. That's according to a new warning from the director of national intelligence about the threat from China. And by the way, a warning that has a rare bipartisan agreement."*

John Ratcliffe, director of National Intelligence: *"China intends to dominate the world, economically, militarily, and technologically. They intend to be the world's superpower."*

MSNBC Reports: *"That's John Ratcliffe, of course, who is out with a new interview and op-ed. The two leaders in both parties on the Senate Intelligence Committee say, basically, he's right that China, 'Will stop at nothing to exert its global dominance.' But here's the part of Ratcliffe's warning that is especially noteworthy. He says China's efforts include human testing to help develop soldiers with those biologically enhanced capabilities, and that is why, of all things, we are talking about super soldiers right now. With me now is Ken Dilanian, who covers national security and intelligence for NBC news. Ken, really, how real is this? How far along is this?"*

Ken Dilanian: *"As you said, Hallie, this does seem like it's right out of a Hollywood plot. But what we know is the nation's top intelligence official say, the US has evidence that China is conducting biological experiments on its soldiers to enhance their capabilities. As you said, he said this as part of an effort to convince Americans about the dire threat to American national security from China. So, I was somewhat skeptical about this* *claim, but when I started poking around, I found that private American military experts in the think tank world have actually studied this issue and written about it. And they have found there is ample evidence that Chinese scientists are very interested in applying biotechnology to the battlefield and specifically, the CRISPR gene editing tool, which raises a ton of questions.*

Picture super strong commandos, who can operate on three hours sleep, or a sniper, who can see twice as far as a normal person. This is the kind of thing that the Chinese aspire to doing, and it's problematic, because in the West we consider it to be unethical to tamper with the genes of healthy people. The CRISPR tool is generally confined to trying to cure genetic mutations and disease and try to improve plants. No one understands the implications of messing with human genes, and so that's a real worry and it also underscores what Ratcliffe and others say, the extent that China is committed to military superiority over the west, Hallie."

MSNBC Reports: *"I want to turn to the China threat. You were really among the first people to come on this program and raise the red flag about China. You told us they were building a very strong military; we know that they've got the largest navy in the world. Well, the director of national intelligence, John Ratcliffe, joined me on Sunday Morning Futures this weekend to talk about the intelligence that shows the Chinese Communist Party and what it's doing."*

John Ratcliffe: *"It's called gene editing. It's altering DNA and it's one of the things our intelligence shows that China is doing. The PRC, the People's Republic of China has two million strong in its military. And it's trying to make them stronger through gene editing. That's just one of the ways China is trying to essentially dominate the planet and set the rules, and the world order. Why it's so important and people need to understand, this is an authoritative regime. It doesn't care about people's individual rights. We've seen what they've done to the Uighurs. We've seen what they've done in Hong Kong. It's about putting the state first, and that is the exact opposite of what has always made America great."*

MSNBC Reports: *"What's your reaction? We've talked about what they're doing and their use of artificial intelligence in the military. But to actually do this gene editing and to have this program to test members of the PLA, two million communists, to try to make them better and more equipped to handle extreme weather, more equipped to handle chemical attacks. Pretty extraordinary the lengths they are going to."*

Ken Dilanian: *"It's not surprising. As Director Ratcliffe said, this is an authoritarian, repressive regime that as a premium is consistently in control of its people. The fact that they are trying to use gene editing tools to change the nature of human beings is not surprising, because this is who they really are. We had the similar experience, did we not, with Nazism, another authoritative regime trying to conduct human experiments to do the very same thing."*

WION Reports: *"If you thought mutant soldiers with unstoppable physical and mental powers were nothing more than science fiction, then brace yourself for what I'm about to tell you. In a chilling op-ed the US intel chief has warned that China could be breeding genetically modified soldiers. You heard that right. The Chinese regime could be creating mutant soldiers. This possibility has been raised by John Ratcliffe, a former Republican Congressman, and the director of national intelligence under the Trump administration. Ratcliffe has released an exhaustive report labeling China as the biggest threat to democracy and freedom since the Second World War.*

He says Beijing is bent on global domination and is giving increasing importance to biotechnology in its military strategy in order to achieve its ambition. He has warned that Chinese authorities have been conducting human tests on members of the People's Liberation army in the hopes of developing soldiers with biologically enhanced capabilities, capabilities like lifting huge weights, infrared night vision, and running at high speeds over extreme distances. Ratcliffe says there seems to be no ethical limits to China's quest for further power. Simon again, several US bases, in fact, have issued similar warnings about soldiers having no physical, psychological, or cognitive limitation.

The sound of gun fire, soldiers marching to defend borders, generals dictating staff picks, that's how we think of war. That's how countries have fought for generations. But what if I told you that everything was about to change. Modern day war is going to be about controlling people's minds, quite literally, and China is making weapons that control minds. I know. Hard to believe, but it's true. China is building such weapons. It's also building biological warfare capabilities. It is conducting influence campaigns. Basically, Beijing is waging unconventional war. It is using every tool in the kit to weaken other nations. What are these tools? Who are the targets? What can the world do to stop China? That's what we discussed.

These brain control weapons. What are they and how did China think of making them? After all, the Chinese are not really known for innovation. Copying is more like their style. How did they come to this one? Here is the story. The United States has an export blacklist. It's a list of companies to whom American businesses cannot export, an export blacklist. Yesterday the U.S. updated this list. They added twelve names, twelve research institutes. One of them is the Academy of Military Medical Sciences, China's top military medical research institute. You could call it the PLA's own science lab. Why has it been blacklisted? Apparently, they conducted a sinister experiment. This institute was helping the Chinese military develop what they call brain control weapons.

I come back to the question, what really is a brain control weapon? Unfortunately, the statement from the United States does not answer that question. But we have some clues to connect the dots. According to one report, China has the need to weaponize biotechnology. They're looking into three areas specifically, gene editing, human performance enhancement, and brain-machine interfaces. Now all of these technologies have one clear military application, which is creating super soldiers. So far, this idea has been limited to superhero movies like the Avengers, humans getting superhuman power capabilities.

But Beijing now wants to make them a reality. One year back, a member of the Trump administration wrote this, and I'm quoting, 'U.S. intelligence *shows that China has even conducted human testing on members of the People's Liberation Army in the hope of developing soldiers with biologically-enhanced capabilities.' What this means is China is getting super soldiers. It is conducting human trials on soldiers, and not even trying to hide this. Three years ago, a paper was published in China. Reports say it was written by PLA euro scientists. The title is self-explanatory, 'Military Brain Science How to Influence Future Wars.' Three years back! America has finally woken up to the threat. It has barred its companies from exporting American technology to Chinese institutions. The point of this report is quite simple. Put all of these inputs together, and you get the big picture. The nature of warfare is changing, and China wants to take the lead to control your mind to win future wars through brain control weapons."*

Wow! Brain control weapons that include not just creating Super Soldiers in North Korea, but openly admitted in China as well. And where did this Covid-19 virus start that then led to the excuse for the Covid-19 shots? That has a programmable payload inside of them, that gives the Global Elites genetic access to people's bodies and brains who took those shots, for who knows what purposes? It all began in China folks! Anybody starting to see a pattern here?

But, hey, good thing we're going to put a stop to this here in the U.S. I mean, we're the voice of moral reason in all this wicked behavior and, surely, we're going to blow the whistle on all this Super Soldier genetically modified technology and put a stop to it before it's too late, right? Wrong. We're doing the exact same thing and we have been for quite some time now. Check out this proof.

Arris Quinones: *"Since all of us were kids, we've always been told by our parents that what we see in comics isn't real. For instance, when I was six, I tried crawling off the second-floor banister, and my mom yelled at me, 'What do think, you're Spiderman or something? Get off that! Spiderman's not real.' But today, I'm going to talk about DARPA, the Defense Advanced Research Projects Agency and how they're working on* *making soldiers into pretty much real-life superheroes. So, take that, parents!*

Like I just mentioned, the Defense Advanced Research Projects Agency is working on a super soldier program, a $300 billion super soldier program, to be exact. The project got started to help make a metabolically dominant soldier. So, in layman's terms, the military is telling us how to use technology and biology to combine man, machine, and science to transcend the limits of the human body. The project director was actually quoted saying, 'My measure of success is that the International Olympic Committee bans everything we do.' So, basically, he wants to create soldiers that are so beyond any normal personal limits, they would be considered superhuman and therefore wouldn't be allowed to compete in the Olympics, which is a little scary and a dream come true, all at the same time. Because, yes, we have real life Captain America, but let's face it. It's only a matter of time before it ends up in the wrong hands, and, boom, we have real-life super villains.

As far as what they are working on, they're working on gear, gadgets and suits that are things Tony Stark would make. The wearer of the gear would be able to run at a hundred meter an hour Olympic sprinter speeds for hours on end, along with giving the person a seven-foot vertical leap. The capability of wall crawling, which being the huge Spiderman fan that I am, I say, heck yes to that one. Also, flight and enhanced strength, which is probably the two top things people would want when asked what superpowers they could have, not to mention invisibility and being able to carry huge weapons on your back. Kinda like War-Machines.

But I did say this was the super soldier program, meaning they're trying to alter the genes within our bodies to make genes stronger and superhuman without the help of gadgets. I meant what I said, because I don't lie, and also because they're doing just that. They're working on drugs and genetic enhancement and some technology that would allow for regeneration just like lizards from Spiderman, fast healing just like Wolverine, and enhanced strength just like Captain America. And even something that would make you like the god of thunder, Thor. We could operate without sleep for days without lack of performance. They're even talking about fixing your cells so that you could live off your fat, which sounds gross, but is cool at the same time.

One of my favorite things they're developing is something that's straight out of Marvel Comic Shield. They're making new body armor that's filled with nano materials that are connected to a computer. It's basically computer-controlled liquid armor. It would normally be as flexible as regular uniform made fabric, but like how airbags work in car crashes, it would activate when the system detects a bullet strike it turns hard as steel in an instant. The fabric could even be woven into nano muscle fibers that would simulate real muscles giving the soldiers an estimated 25-35 percent better lifting capabilities. So pretty much what I'm saying, Lucius Fox works for DARPA.

In conclusion, it looks like Stan Lee and all the other great minds of comics are right, and our parents wrong. What's also a major focus is helping soldiers' bodies to deal better with trauma and physical injury. One idea in development is a pain vaccine. Researchers are hopeful that these vaccines will be able to block the senses of pain for almost a month. It would block the pain in less than ten seconds. So, let's say you're in war and you get stabbed. You'd only feel the pain for less than ten seconds, before the vaccine kicks in, then, boom, no more pain. It supposedly doesn't stifle your reactions either. If you were to touch a hot stove, you still would have the initial shock. Your hand would automatically jerk away, but after that the pain would be gone.

Doctors say it has already hit its first milestone in animal testing. And are preparing, of course, for scientific conferences."

Newscaster: *"The soldier of the future won't just be battle-trained and ready to kill. They'll be genetically engineered to withstand a biological attack. The Pentagon has a plan for editing the DNA and creating super soldiers."*

Steven Walker, US Defense Advanced Research Projects Agency Director: *"Why is Defense Advanced Research Projects Agency doing this? To protect the soldier on the battlefield from chemical weapons and biological weapons by controlling their genome, having the genome produce proteins that would automatically protect the soldier from the inside out."*

Newscaster: *"So far this sounds a little bit closer to science fiction, perhaps a bit more fantasy than fact."*

Tommy Lee Jones in Captain America movie: "He will be the first in a new breed of super soldiers…" The clip shows how he was injected with this chemical weapon and how he was able to be strong enough to lead and fight with his group.

Newscaster: *"Earlier this year, a Chinese scientist announced that two girls were born with edited genomes. Genomes that were edited to be HIV resistant. So, with potentially boundless possibilities, the question now is, what altered genes would a US soldier need?"*

People on the street discuss this with RT Reports: *"Probably put some brains in them, so they could question the policies."*

"They're already good soldiers. I think how God created them is good enough for me."

"Are you kidding me? Well, I'm asking you, because that's the most outrageous thing I've ever heard."

"The benefits of DNA could be used to live longer, be happier, maybe be less reliant on things like, I don't know, waste? Why do we use this for soldiers?"

RT Reports: *"You don't like the idea?"*

"No, I don't."

"That's sad, because there's gotta be consequences to that."

"Oh, I'd change their strength, their vision, anything that would make them a better soldier, I suppose."

Newscaster: *"But before you let your imagination run too wild, remember the US military says there is no need to worry. It's all for a good cause."*

Steven Walker, US Defense Advanced Research Projects Agency Director: *"All these technologies, they are dual use. You can use them for good, and you can use them for evil. The Defense Advanced Research Projects Agency is about using them for good to protect our warfighters."*

Newscaster: *"The potential of genetic engineering should not be underestimated. There is a lot that can be done beyond simply fire-breathing, always-on, fully weaponized, warriors. Keep your eyes out for the genetically modified soldiers of the future. Unlike GMO food they may not always be labeled.*

In other words, you may not even know they're right next to you. Is this insane, or what? First North Korea, then China, and apparently, it's been going on for quite some time, even here in America as well. What kind of sick world are we headed for? Well, it's not just sick, it's dangerous. Because pretty much all developed countries are developing their own Super Soldiers to the point where even Vladimir Putin, of all people, of Russia said, *"This is more dangerous than a nuclear bomb."*

Vladimir Putin: *"Mankind has become capable of interfering with the genetic code created by nature or, according to religious people, created by God. What are the possible consequences of that? One can almost imagine that people will be able to create human beings with specific characteristics. This person can be a brilliant mathematician or a brilliant musician, but also a soldier – a human being capable of fighting without fear, without compassion, without regret, or even pain. You see, humanity can enter, and most likely will enter in the near future into a very difficult period of its development and existence, a period demanding great* *responsibility. And what I have just described may be worse than a nuclear bomb. Whenever we do something and whatever it is that we do, we should never forget about the ethical and moral foundations behind our actions."*

Yeah, no kidding. But that's not stopping these Global Elites from doing what they're doing! And as crazy as all this sounds, if you want even more evidence on this Super Soldier technology and genetic modification issue from various countries around the world, again, get our other documentary, ***Human Hybrids, Super Soldiers & the Coming Genetic Apocalypse***. We trace the whole trail all throughout history of how we got here today with what you just saw and how it all came about.

Chapter Nine

The Zombies of Human 2.0

But let's go on to the next statement made by Todd Callender in The Corona Investigative Committee Interview. If you recall in the last segment, he brought up a very disturbing piece of information. If you caught it there, he said all this genetic manipulation technology could even "reanimate organisms" from the dead, and they already did these kinds of experiments on animals. You know, making Zombies? But wait a second. That can't be true, can it? Well, let's take a look at what else Todd shares.

Viviane Fischer: *"If we're looking at normal mortality for these creatures, I have two questions. Do you think they are, would they still be like breeding, like traditional human beings? And how are they included in this kind of program? Are they really included? I mean the ones who are behind all this. I mean the ones who pull the strings. Do you think, they like to stay normal human beings? Or is this not what they want?"*

Todd Callender: *"I don't know the answer to that. My sense is they do have a goal of immortality. How they achieve that immortality, I do not know. And that's another thing we could look up with Craig Bestor. What I do understand is they want limited resources on this planet. They've been very clear about that. Bill Gates has said we want to get that number down to zero. Georgia Guidestones says no more than 500 million. You* *look at the sustainable development goals, they want a 95% reduction in world population. So, as to the owners, my suspicion is they'll want immortality. I don't know if they'll want the rest of the superpowers or not.*

The Bible talks about it, too. Those that take the mark of the beast will seek to die and not be able too. So, as to people who receive the shots, are they going to be human or die? The answer is, I don't think so. One other thing to be aware of is that in the nano particles there is also the delivery of CRISPR technology, which is a gene-deletion program. If you look at the curious adverse events of that event of Pfizer on their post-marketing study that came out of the FOIA request that they had to disclose, the number one serious adverse event that came up was the 1P36 gene deletion syndrome, that is a congenital disease that causes the loss of your frontal cortex, that's your reasoning, and thinking behavior. It causes facial tics. It causes biting episodes and things of that nature.

So, the only way a person who wasn't born with that to get it is because there was a gene deletion that occurred in their body. It also appears that they eliminated the VMAT2, which is the 'god gene' and the PAT5 which is also related to people's spirituality. So, it appears that those who got those peculiar gene-deletion proteins, they will not be thinking. They will act very zombie like, in fact, they will have spiritually, no connection to God, no remorse, no conscience whatsoever."

Viviane Fischer: *"Some people say that they notice, some doctors or healers say they notice different behavior with their patients after the shot. They may be more aggressive or less facial features. They just like blink. You don't get what they're saying. Also, some healers told me they're not able to, kind of, even reach this person anymore on a spiritual or energetic level. Do you think this is also connected to what you just said?"*

Todd Callender: *"I do. I would highly suspect that those persons had already suffered the 1P36 gene deletion syndrome. What you described is the very behavior that you would see as a result of that.*

Exoneration, to be very clear with you, what we do know is that these people are really good at predictive programming. How many zombie movies have you seen in your life? If you look at Conplan8888, it's the US government plan in case of a zombie apocalypse. They describe five different types of zombies that they might encounter. Every US agency that is mission compliant, that has had to provide robust protection for their computer systems, has undergone zombie apocalypse invasions.

The CDC has had a zombie apocalypse preparedness page up on their website for the last five years. Now they've turned it into a cartoon. You go to Amazon webster's agreement you'll see there is a force majeure part if there is a zombie apocalypse, we're not liable. There's too much talk about zombies for us to ignore the fact that the 1P36 gene dilution combined with the VMAT2-PAT5 dilution creates a zombie-like effect in people. I think that they're just telling us what they're going to do. Click on your 18 GHtz signal and, bang, you got a Marburg zombie apocalypse in progress."

Viviane Fischer: *"I think this could also be, like I read that they claimed that this is just for educational purposes and really just to get you interested. And to do like a strategic game type of thing, might be a pretext or it could also be like real, and they want to drag you into it."*

Todd Callender: *"I can absolutely guarantee you, if you were to look at Conplan8888 you will see on the second page they say exactly what you just said, this is just for the purposes of exercise. The problem with that, I'm ex-military. I represent any and all of these people in the military. I understand how the preparation for war works. You practice where you're going to fight and who you're going to fight. Always. If you look at the ComPlan8888, it has nothing to do with fighting Ecuador or other countries, it has to do with fighting five different types of genetically modified zombies. Some are vaccine zombies, some are radiation zombies, some are magic zombies. They have five different types of zombies. And they are preparing and practicing to fight. It has nothing to do with territory. It has nothing to do with ideology or insurgency. Its only about* *zombies. So, I understand what it is you are saying, I don't believe it for a second."*

Viviane Fischer: *"Is that already something that's going to be new stuff? Like ever evolving, what they will then give to the people?"*

Todd Callender: *"I think so. In March, I think it's actually March of 22, I'll send you the convention they had in Texas, a convention on the commercialization of these liquid nano particles. I'm also going to send you the NASA warfare plan and its N-A-S-A, because they talk about the use of these liquid nano particles being able to be crop dusted. They fly over these cities, they drop the nano particles, they get into people's lungs, and they burrow in and control the population. This is the stuff they talk about. This convention they had on the 22nd of March was to share the knowledge and technology of commercialization, mass production of these liquid nano particles. Whatever passages, whatever payloads you have to have in such numbers they literally now could be exactly as you described. They could fly over a city and turn everybody into whatever they want to happen. They can do that now.*

Second host: *"So, it's not the Sahara dust, it's nano particles. Nanobots. So, we could easily analyze the dust and find out."*

Todd Callender: *"That's a great idea. I think it's a super idea. It's not like they've been hiding it. They've been talking about smart dust for ages. That definitely exists. I think you won't have a hard time finding it."*

Second host: *"But as long as they have billions of people vaccinated or injected, they needn't spray something in the air. They just give it directly into the people."*

Todd Callender: *"I think so. I don't know exactly why it is. My sense is they needed to install the hardware in people first. There are thirty-three hundred commercial products, foods, they already have the nano particles in them. If you're drinking a Pepsi or a Coke, you're ingesting these nano particles. They're everywhere. But for whatever reason, our bodies seem* *o have the abilities to repel these. Our natural immunity. So, my sense is, 'n order to be the hardware installation, they have to get the HIV protein 'n order to disarm our natural immunity. That was the key part of these shots. And thereafter I suppose they can deliver their shots or upgrades as 'hey want too. But what's probably most efficient is to shoot them in with a shot."*

Dr. Reiner Fuellmich: *"Well, that is quite a horror show."*

Todd Callender: *"Yeah, it is. I'm sorry that's the case. I'm going to send you a lot of information that backs up everything I said."*

Dr. Reiner Fuellmich: *"Please do that. We have to do this. As horrific as this is, we have to know about it. We have to get into the details of this. In order to be able to, well, at least get an idea of how dangerous, it's obviously very, very dangerous and what we can do about it."*

Yeah, I agree, what can we do about it, which is precisely why we are doing this. The first step is to educate people. But just when you thought it couldn't get any worse with these Covid shots, it just did, infinitely so! Now Todd is exposing that these genetically modified shots can also turn people into Zombies. Real life Zombies? Are you serious? I mean, surely, that's not a part of the Global Elites plan, is it? Well, let's go back to the "reanimation" part. Is Reanimation Technology a viable reality? Let's take a look at that.

TomoNews Reports: *"It's taken nearly two decades, but scientists may finally have the recipe to create stem cells, that wellspring of life and holy grail of regenerative medicine. A Boston research team programmed human pluripotent stem cells to become endopleura cells, which typically line the inside of blood vessels. These were injected with special proteins called transcription factors then transplanted into mice. Weeks later the cells had multiplied and, in some cases, formed a wide range of human blood cells in the mice bodies.*

A second research team used blood cells from mice and injected them with a mix of transcription factors. The cells morphed into stem cells after incubating in petri dishes designed to mimic a human blood vessel environment. When injected into weak mice that had been treated with radiation, the stem cells regenerated both blood and immune cells. The mice recovered and went on to live full life spans.

Researchers at Ohio State University have developed a new technology that allows the body to generate any type of cell to help heal injuries. Tissue nano-transfection involves placing a fingernail size nano chip on a patient's skin adding a droplet of genetic material and zapping it with an electrical current. The DNA is delivered through channels created by the current and it reprograms skin cells to turn into specific cell types that can then be used in other parts of the body. When tested on a mouse with a damaged leg, researchers found vascular cells converted from skin cells, formed new blood vessels that allowed the leg to heal in two weeks.

The non-invasive technology was also able to generate nerve cells in the legs of brain-damaged mice. Once the cells were harvested, they were injected into the brain to help with stroke recovery. The nano-chip also tested effectively with pigs. And is expected to be approved for human trials in a year."

Now imagine if you could get that nanotechnology on the inside of people, say with a Covid injection, and voila! Notice it responded to "an electronic signal" to activate it, and you can do all kinds of things, including "reanimation." Anybody seeing a pattern here? The technology to "reanimate" things is already here! But wait a second. Are the Global Elites really looking at using this "reanimation" technology to "reanimate" people?

Well, let's take a look again at their propaganda machine, also known as Hollywood. What kind of future are we headed for? According to Hollywood, with all this nanotechnology, we're really going to be "reanimating" people.

The clip from the movie "Blood Shot" opens with a man, maybe a scientist turning on a radio. The song playing is "Memories are made of this."

Scientist: *"Initiate sequence."*

Vin Diesel: *"Jenna I'm home."*

They seem very happy. They seem to be in a tropical paradise. Suddenly, he awakens in a cold dark room strapped to a cold slab in the middle of the floor.

Vin Diesel: *"What is this place?"*

Scientist: *"I'm sorry to be the one to tell you this, but you got yourself killed."*

The scientist proceeds to take Vin Diesel around the complex to explain what is going on.

Scientist: *"At RST, we rebuild the most important asset in the U.S. military, soldiers like yourself. You're the first that we've successfully managed to bring back. But improved, enhanced, with the technology in your veins, you have an army inside you. It will not only make you stronger, but it will also heal you instantly. Now tell me, do you remember anything?"*

The music starts playing again, and he is back with his wife. But that memory fades and a new one comes into his mind. He is strapped to a chair looking at his wife. She is strapped to another chair in front of him and a man is standing next to her with a gun pointed at her head. He is remembering something that is now making him a warrior to do their bidding. His wife was murdered in front of his eyes.

The scientist's assistant asks him: *"Where are you going?"*

Vin Diesel: *"I've got unfinished business. I've got to find the man who murdered my wife and kill him."*

He proceeds to go on the hunt for this man that killed his wife, but, in the process, he is a war machine and is tearing up and killing everyone that gets in his way.

Scientist: *"Oh, that's not good. Alright, shut him down and initiate the sequence."*

When he hears the music, he collapses on the floor. His memories take him back with his wife once again.

Scientist: *"OK, who is the next target for elimination?"*

While he thinks he is back with his wife in paradise, they are putting wires to his head and continuing with their experiment. And they put a new person with a new memory in his head for him to eliminate.

Scientist: *"Tell me. Do you remember anything?"*

Vin Diesel: *"Do I know you guys?"*

Scientist: *"I don't think so. What do you think is real?"*

Vin Diesel has found another warrior soldier being held in the complex. That warrior tells him *"Sometimes I ..."*

"And initiate sequence." The music begins to play. Being a hero is in his blood.

They keep questioning him to make sure he doesn't get out of control.

Vin Diesel: *"You can't control me forever."*

Scientist: *"You sure about that? Revenge is what makes a man like you exceptional."*

Vin Diesel: *"You know nothing about men like me."*

Scientist: *"This guy is absolutely fantastic."*

As the music starts playing again Vin Diesel says: *"I feel like I just heard this, are they playing this on repeat?"*

Notice, the title of that movie…*Blood Shot*. Once they get that nanotechnology inside the bloodstream, you know, like with the Covid shot, they can do all kinds of things to people, even reanimate you. But wait a second, they aren't really looking at using nanotechnology inside of humans like in that movie premise to regenerate and reanimate things and who knows what else with all that nanotechnology inside of them from the Covid shots are they?

Well, let's take a look at what the Global Elites and their scientific community are telling us really is coming for those who received the "injectable" nanobots.

Bertalan Meska, MD, PhD: *"You are living in the dawn of the nanomedicine age. Nanoparticles and nanodevices will soon operate as precise drug delivery systems, cancer treatment tools, or tiny surgeons. Let me introduce you to the brave new world of nanotechnology in healthcare.*

You might remember a few years ago, British sculptor, Willard Wigan went viral with his micro sculptures on needles. Look how small they are compared to even a common housefly. But compared to the nanometer, the basic unit of measurement in nanotechnology, these are still huge. A nanometer is a million times smaller than the length of an ant. A sheet of paper is about one hundred thousand nanometers thick. It's basically atomic and molecular level.

*When I was a kid, one of my favorite TV series was a French animation,
Once Upon a Time... Life. I found it fascinating how the creators
imagined the human body as a construction where tiny cars floated
through the human veins, and bacteria as tiny monsters tried to attack
innocent screaming lady cells, while white blood cells defended the body
as well-trained soldiers.*

*Now imagine that all this could happen in real life. Nanotechnology
comprises science, engineering and technology conducted at the nano
scale. And we are more advanced at it than you think. For example,
researchers from the Max Planck Institute have been experimenting with
exceptionally micro-sized, smaller than millimeter, robots, that literally
swim through your body fluids and could be used to deliver drugs in a
hydra way. These scallop-like micro bots are designed to swim through
non-Newtonian fluids, like your blood stream, around your lymphatic
system or across the slippery goo on the surface of your eyeballs. And as
this technology will get more advanced, it has the possibility to turn
healthcare upside down.*

*Let's take a look at a few more examples. Nanotechnology has the
potential to revolutionize the way we collect medical data. With nano sized
diagnostic devices throughout our bodies, we will be able to detect
chemical changes on the spot. These devices could be programmed into
gathering information about certain body parts, levels of toxins, and other
substances, and report back to medical professionals or to its hosts. In the
future, it might become a reality that the nano robot sends others to their
smartphone about the changes it detects. This allows for detection of
diseases and real-time tracking of a patient's health status.*

*Imagine programmable nanoparticles which could help tackle the day-to-
day miseries of chronic conditions, like diabetes. For example, they could
deliver insulin to initiate cell growth and regenerate tissue at a target
location. They could also be programmed to bring certain substances to
cells or could be injected into the bloodstream to seek out and remove
damaged cells or grow new cells. The traditional method for curing
cancer is chemotherapy, that's usually described as a carpet bombing of*

he body. In many cases it kills the cancer cell, but it also has a side effect of killing regular cells, which makes patients extremely sick and susceptible to other conditions. But programmable nanoparticles that attack cancer cells directly without damaging other tissues could mean a revolution in cancer treatment. It's more like a tomahawk precision missile. It would be an amazing addition to our arsenal against cancer.

Nanotechnology has made it possible for researchers to collect in-depth data on the human brain by using nano-scale diamond particles. The brain's activities are converted into frequencies of light that can be registered by external sensors, allowing researchers to study the brain in much greater detail. With microscopic size of just a billionth of a millimeter, nanoparticles are able to cross the blood-brain barrier and access the brain's remote areas.

They have also shown tremendous potential in being a useful alternative to diagnosing and treating neurological diseases. According to optimistic futurists, nanomedicines - like smart drugs - will lead to the prevention of illnesses, even aging, making us superhuman. But it's time for the medical community regulators and the public to start to catch up, because the nano future is upon us.

Sound familiar? That looks like some of the side effects of people who took the Covid shots. But wait a second, what if all this nano injection technology goes wrong? What's this going to do to people other than the side effects we just saw?

Well, again, let's get back to the Global Elites propaganda machine, you know, Hollywood, and see if they're preparing us for some sort of "genetic manipulation scenario gone wrong." You know, a Zombie attack.

First of all, Zombie movies are everywhere!

Hundreds and hundreds of them! Which blows me away because they used to be just Grade "B," goofy black and white comical movies, back in the 50's and 60's. But now, they're everywhere with people being totally infatuated with them. Apparently, their propaganda is paying off!

There's Zombie festivals, Zombie walks, Zombie clothing, Zombie wear, Zombie this, Zombie that, Zombies are everywhere! Why? Well, maybe like what Todd Callender said, it's to prepare us for what's coming with these genetically modified shots people received! You send out the right "electronic signal," and, voila, just like that, you got a whole population of Zombies all over the place, instantly. You know, like this propaganda film portrays. I warn you, it's a little graphic.

Hideo Suzuki, a Manga artist assistant, is drawing with his co-workers in the office, listening to the news. A news reporter is describing an incident in which a dog badly bit a 45-year-old woman. The police couldn't figure out what exactly happened, because the woman started talking nonsense after the accident. The next news story is about a 35-year-old man who was arrested because of performing an obscene act. One co-worker notices how news is becoming weird, and Mitani, a co-worker, makes fun of Suzuki and Manga artists. Suzuki then explains how Manga is the peak of Japanese culture, and that it is an honor to be a Manga artist. He motivates the other co-workers, and everybody yells, "Manga is the best!"

Night comes, and Suzuki arrives home. In his apartment, he watches TV with Tekko, his passive-aggressive girlfriend, and draws. He looks at his Manga award and motivational quotes like "The steep jobs of Manga world and the road to Manga is harsh."

Suzuki looks for inspiration for his next comic. So, he takes a rifle from his cupboard and looks at himself in the mirror.

In the morning, everybody is sick and coughing at the publisher's office, where Suzuki is showing

his new Manga comic about a macho guy protecting his girlfriend with a rifle. The publisher doesn't like the comic. He says the protagonist is too normal and tells Suzuki to do a better job in the future. Then, another Manga artist, Sensei, sees Suzuki. Sensei is more popular than him but shared the new Manga artist award with Suzuki fifteen years ago.

Later, in his apartment, Suzuki is fighting with Tekko, who wants to sell the rifle so, they can get at least some money and pay rent. She also wants to sell his award along with his Manga books. Tekko is sick of Suzuki's failures and his unfulfilled dreams of becoming the next best Manga artist. So, in a fit of rage, she breaks up with him and kicks him out of the apartment.

Suzuki then goes to the park with his gun and starts looking at Sensei's comic book. Sitting next to him is a homeless man who is shaking, and looks like he is pain, but Suzuki doesn't pay any special attention.

The next morning, Suzuki is in his office, with his co-workers, drawing and watching the news again. There is a report about a new infection that has already killed four people. Suzuki's colleague is sweating and not feeling well. She leaves and Mitani explains to the others how she got the virus from Sensei. Mitani notices how she had the same bite mark on the neck as Sensei. That is how he figured out they were sleeping together. Their boss enters the room, and he also has a bite mark. They are confused and ask him about the deadline, but don't notice his eyes getting darker.

Later, everybody is asleep at the office when Suzuki's phone suddenly rings. It's Tekko, who apologizes for last night and wants to continue their relationship. While talking on the phone, helicopters pass over the city. But Suzuki is too focused on Tekko and doesn't pay attention. He immediately goes to Tekko's flat, bringing her favorite snack. He begs her to open the door. Nobody answers so he tries calling her on the phone. Suzuki peeks through the letter slot and sees Tekko laying on the bed. Suddenly she gets up, making weird movements, and drops on the floor. Next thing we know, she's having a seizure while her body morphs unnaturally, like a demon during an exorcism. As she approaches the door, Suzuki sees her face is deformed. Zombie Tekko attacks Suzuki and bites his hand. While trying to get away, he accidentally stabs her in the head (with his award laying on the floor, she falls on it)

and leaves the apartment, fast.

As he is crossing the bridge, he notices a woman with a bleeding hand, and then dozens of airplanes flying through the city.

When he returns to the office, Suzuki sees Mitani standing next to the TV with his back turned. Suzuki thinks he is a zombie too, but then sees him holding a bloody baseball bat. So, he quietly enters the office where the rest of his co-workers are dead zombies, and Mitani is the only survivor. He tells Suzuki that the only way to kill zombies is to destroy their brains, and those who get bit, get infected. But it turns out Mitani is bitten too, and when he starts turning into a zombie, he kills himself, screaming, "The era of underpaid workers has arrived since all their bosses are now dead zombies." Another infected worker arrives, and Suzuki quickly leaves the office.

In the streets, half the people aren't even aware of what's going on. Some are walking casually down the street, while others are running. Within a few minutes people start realizing that demonic looking zombies are among them. Some start to run, while others fall prey to the hungry

zombies. Suzuki desperately approaches a police officer, but the policeman is a zombie too, and starts chasing him. Suzuki is running away as fast as he can, when, suddenly, he stops to watch a large group of people running in one direction. Cars are bumping into each other. City buildings are burning, and people are getting run over by ambulance cars. In all that mess, Suzuki notices a cab driver who is sleeping in the taxi and is completely unaware of the zombie apocalypse. Before entering inside, Hiromi, a high school student, approaches him. She wants to get into the taxi, as well, but a zombie talking on the phone attacks them.

Suzuki imagines he is taking out his rifle and aiming at the zombie. So, he is standing frozen, shooting with his fingers instead. At the same time, a man in a suit wants to take their taxi. They start to bang on the car windows and luckily manage to get into the taxi as well, instructing the driver to drive towards the countryside. On the cab TV, the news reports the attacks as riots. It's obvious that no one has answers. So, they switch to Tokyo TV and see an Anime cartoon being broadcast. Suzuki thinks Tokyo is safe, because they are showing the anime, but soon the channel ends the cartoon and starts reporting the attacks.

As they are watching, the guy in the business suit is talking on the phone, instructing someone to shoot everyone. Even the Prime Minister, if necessary. When he hangs up, he starts complaining about the poor. And suddenly he reveals a bite on his arm. His blood vessels quickly turn

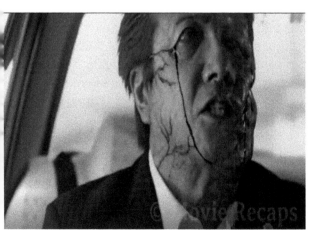

black. He's turning into a zombie while saying, "Hey, poor people, give me a tissue." The taxi driver isn't aware that the businessman is turning into a zombie, so he gives him a tissue. The new zombie then bites him. The driver opens the car door, and Suzuki manages to push *out the zombie. Everybody breathes a sigh of relief, when the taxi driver's veins start to turn black too. He starts telling them how he was an excellent taxi driver for thirty years, with no car accidents. Then, he gets angry about it and starts driving like a mad man. Hiromi goes to the back seat, and it's lucky she does, because the taxi driver soon starts attacking them. Suzuki and Hiromi put on their seatbelts, because the car is going at a high speed. Soon, they crash into another car and start tumbling. When Suzuki wakes up, the car is turned over, but Hiromi is alive. When they leave the car, they see how the entire road is blocked, because of a massive car collision. All the cars are empty, and there's nobody on the road.*

So, Suzuki and Hiromi sit on the sidewalk and start browsing the internet to find out what's going on. They read how the virus is named ZQN and how it corrupts the personalities and bodies of the infected.

Yeah, and I wonder how that happened all over the world, all of a sudden, simultaneously. Gee, good thing that was just a movie! Maybe, maybe not. Remember, Hollywood is a propaganda machine, and whether this Zombie Apocalypse reality the Global Elites are preparing us for with their propaganda machine known as Hollywood is from "genetic experiments" gone wrong or done to people on purpose to create yet another global crisis, on top of all the other possibilities, so they can take even more power and control from people across the planet, I don't know.

But what I do know is that the Global Elites and governments around the world are really preparing for a Zombie-type Apocalypse, just like Todd Callender said. Let's put his words to the test again. He said they already had plans in place with the CDC and even the Pentagon to deal with a Zombie Apocalypse. Is that true? Let's check it out.

Narrator: *"In 2011, the CDC published a plan outlining how the public should equip themselves for and respond to a zombie apocalypse... recommending that everyone keep a kit with 3 days of food and water enough time to find a "zombie-free refugee camp."*

Families were advised to establish a meeting place and evacuation plan to be able to flee to safety and avoid infection.

A zombie invasion would be treated like an outbreak with the CDC conducting lab tests and controls, including quarantines and interviewing zombies (if possible) to determine the source of the infection and understand how it is transmitted. Later, the CDC inexplicably backtracked, claiming it 'does not know of a virus or condition that would reanimate the dead.'

Pentagon document, 'Conplan8888-11 Counter-zombie Dominance,' outlines the U.S. government's zombie invasion response plan. Though created as a training thought experiment, the plan explicitly states that it is 'not designed as a joke' and has three objectives: protect humankind from zombies, eradicate zombie threats, and maintain order during a zombie attack. Several variants of zombie lifeforms are identified, including space, symbiont-induced, radiation, and weaponized zombies. The plan concludes the only way to defeat a zombie is by "concentration of all firepower to the head, specifically the brain."

The Pentagon alarmingly acknowledged that it currently has 'no ground combat forces capable of repelling a zombie assault' and that military command centers would likely be overrun 'within the first days of a zombie invasion.' The 'National Emergency Operations' section of the IRS's Internal Revenue Manual outlines its operations in an apocalyptic scenario.

Should the IRS's facilities be compromised, a makeshift emergency operations center will be established wherever possible from which 'operations will be concentrated on collecting the taxes which will produce the greater revenue yield.' Surviving employees would be expected to assume any role necessary to resume tax collection within 30 days of an outbreak.

The revenue will be essential for funding a robust zombie counterattack and eradication strategy by the U.S. government. The manual anticipates

*poor people will be 'most adversely affected,' leaving the wealthy to
continue paying taxes.*

*With his equation (bN)(S/N)Z = bSZ, Robert J. Smith created a
mathematical model to determine the best zombie survival strategy. N
representing the total population, S the number of susceptible people, Z
the zombies, and b the likelihood of transmission. Smith's
'catastrophizing' models determined that 'a zombie outbreak is likely to
lead to the collapse of civilization.' He concluded that a popular method
of combating zombies via quarantine would only 'delay the time to
eradication of humans.'*

*Should we quickly develop a cure for 'zombie-ism,' survival is possible but
in the end humans will 'only exist in low numbers.' According to Smith,
'the most effective way to contain the rise of the undead is through force –
'hit hard and hit often!'*

Looks to me like a multitude of Government agencies are
preparing for a Zombie Apocalypse, just like Todd Callender said. And
just like they've been preparing us for, in the movies, for many years now.
And could this be another reason why the Seven-Year Tribulation is going
to be such a horrible time frame? As we saw earlier Jesus said it's the
worst time in the history of mankind.

Matthew 24:21-22 "For then there will be great distress, unequaled from
the beginning of the world until now – and never to be equaled again. If
those days had not been cut short, no one would survive."

Yeah, maybe everybody would be a Zombie. And maybe Todd
was right after all when he was quoting the following passage of Scripture
that speaks of those who in the Seven-Year Tribulation take the Mark of
the Beast.

Revelation 9:6 "During those days men will seek death but will not find
it; they will long to die, but death will elude them."

Gee, I wonder how that could happen? Maybe they just keep "reanimating." I don't know. But as you can see, as sick and shocking and horrific as all this is, this really is what these Global Elites have planned for us. And maybe it will also be as Todd Callender warns, "It would give them the ability to shut us off, i.e., a human kill switch, where when they don't need us anymore, they just kill us, right there on the spot with a "signal," when they deem us no longer necessary."

But what we do know is they audaciously tell us about these wicked plans in advance for those who have eyes to see and ears to hear. These plans are not good, and they very well, as shocking as it sounds, could involve everything we just talked about in this book.

And that is even more Plandemics, treating us like Human Cattle, creating Super Soldiers for their army, and even unleashing Zombie-like humans, either on purpose or by genetic accident, to create an even bigger crisis in the future that will cause even more death and destruction and be used as an excuse to grab even more control over the rest of the survivors on the planet.

Chapter Ten

The Response to Human 2.0

Now, as sick, and satanic as those plans are, Lord willing, this is what we will be dealing with in even greater detail in our next two documentaries.

Klaus Schwab, the World Economic Forum & the Coming Great Reset

As well as…

Elon Musk: Technological Savior or Co-laborer of the Antichrist?

But here's a little teaser of where we will be headed in those two documentaries, straight from the horse's mouth. It's not good folks. Check it out.

What is the 4th Industrial Revolution?

Klaus Schwab: *"The 4th Industrial Revolution will impact our lives completely. It will not only change how we communicate, how we produce, how we consume, it will actually change us, our own identity, and of course gives life to such courtesies and developments, like Smart Traffic,*

Smart Government, Smart Cities. What you will see is that everything will be integrated into an ecosystem driven by big data and driven particularly by close cooperation, also of governments with business and civil society.

This revolution will come at great breaking speed. It will be like a tsunami. Actually, it's not just a digital revolution. It's digital, of course physical, its nanotechnology, but it's also biological."

Interviewer: *"Today, at the end of this, we are talking about chips that can be implanted. When will that be?"*

Klaus Schwab: *Certainly, in the next ten years. And at first, we will implant them in our clothes. And then we could imagine that we will implant them in our brains, or in our skin. And in the end, maybe, there will be a direct communication between our brain and the digital world."*

Erik Brynjolfsson, Massachusetts Institute of Technology (MIT), USA: *"We are now in the early stages of the 4th Industrial Revolution, which is bringing together digital, physical, and biological systems."*

Klaus Schwab: *"One of the features of the 4th Industrial Revolution is it doesn't change what we are doing, but it changes us."*

Yuval Noah Harari, a lead advisor for Klaus Schwab. Yuval has been praised by Barack Obama, Bill Gates, Mark Zuckerberg, TED, the New York Times: *"We don't need to wait for Jesus Christ to come back to earth in order to overcome death. A couple of geeks in a laboratory can do it.*

We will have the possibility of upgrading humans into superhumans. We are giving up on God, but we will turn ourselves into new kinds of gods. We may be able to acquire divine abilities to ourselves.

In the next few decades, we are likely to see the emergence of non-organic life, the greatest revolution not only in history, but also in biology. The

21st Century when they see the emergence of a new massive class of useless people, people who have absolutely no economic value."

Klaus Schwab: *"With all the current issues on our agenda, we tend to forget that we are in the midst of the 4th Industrial Revolution, which accelerates global change in much more comprehensive and faster ways than the previous three revolutions."*

Klaus Schwab: *"You see, the difference of the 4th Industrial Revolution is it doesn't change what you are doing, it changes you. If you take genetic editing, just as an example, it's you who are changed, and of course it has a big impact on your identity."*

Yuval Noah Harari: *"We need to realize that humans are now hackable animals. You can hack them. A good two-way communication system, direct communication system, between brains and computers, this is kind of the watershed moment. Once you have a good two-way, nobody has any idea what happens after that.*

I think maybe in a couple of decades, when people look back, the thing they will remember from the Covid crisis is this is the moment when everything went digital; and this was the moment when everything became monitored, that we agreed to be surveyed all the time. Not just in a totalitarian regime, but even in democracies. And maybe most importantly of all, this was the moment when surveillance started going under the skin.

I think the big process that is happening right now in the world is hacking human beings, the ability to hack humans. To understand deeply what's happening within you. What makes you go. And for that, the most important data is not what you read and who you meet and what you buy, it's what's happening inside your body. So, if we had these two big revolutions, the computer science revolution or the info-tech revolution, and the revolution in the biological sciences, and they are still separate, but they are about to merge."

Klaus Schwab: *"History is truly at a turning point. We do not yet know the full extent and the systemic and structural changes which will happen. However, we do know, the global energy systems, food systems, and supply chains will be deeply affected.*

The 4th Industrial Revolution is actually changing ourselves. It's changing not only what we are doing, it's changing who we are.

At the end, what the 4th Industrial Revolution will lead to is a fusion of our physical, our digital, and our biological identities."

Yuval Noah Harari: *"The whole idea that humans have this soul, or spirit, they have free will, and nobody knows what's happening inside me, so whatever I choose, whether in the election or whether in the supermarket, this is my free will. That's over. We are probably one of the last generations of homo sapiens."*

Joe Rogan: *"If someone ultimately does get a neuralink installed, what will take place?"*

Elon Musk: *"Well, for version one of the device, it would be basically implanted in your skull. So, it would be flush with your skull. So, you are basically, take out a chunk of skull, put the neurologic device in there. You would insert the electro threads very carefully into the brain, and then you stitch it up. You wouldn't even know that somebody has it. It can interface, basically, anywhere in your brain."*

Joe Rogan: *"If you want to get, you know, the real turbocharged version, the P100D of brain stimulation."*

Elon Musk: *"Ultimately, if you want to go with full AI symbiosis, you'll probably want to do something like that."*

Joe Rogan: *"Symbiosis is a scary word when it comes to AI."*

Elon Musk: *"It's optional."*

Joe Rogan: *"I would hope so. It's just, I mean, once you enjoy the doctor Manhattan lifestyle, once you become a god, seems very unlikely you're gonna want to go back to being stupid again. You literally can fundamentally change the way human beings interface with each other."*

Elon Musk: *"Yes. You wouldn't need to talk. You could also save state."*

Joe Rogan: *"Save state?"*

Elon Musk: *"Save your brain state. Like save game, in a video game."*

Joe Rogan: *"Wow! Like if you want to swap from Windows 95."*

Elon Musk: *"Something better than that."*

Joe Rogan: *"I think we are Windows 95 right now."*

Elon Musk: *"From your perspective, probably. But, yeah, you could save state, and restore that state into a biological being if you wanted to. There is nothing from a physical standpoint that prevents us. You'd be a little different, but you're a little different when you wake up in the morning from yesterday.*

I think there are going to be a lot of breakthroughs on the medical front. Particularly around synthetic mRNA. You can basically do anything with synthetic RNA, DNA. It's like a computer program. You could probably stop aging, reverse it if you want. You can turn somebody into a freaking butterfly if you want, with the right DNA sequence."

Wow! Not looking too bright for our future! Those are some pretty sick, smirky smiles these Global Elites are dishing out at us, while talking about the future that they're building for us. Can you believe what they have planned? As you can see, it's not good. And believe it or not, in their own words, they even admit to having these sick, satanic, human-altering plans in place, around the whole planet, by 2030. That's their goal! But stay tuned for those next two documentaries, Lord willing, coming soon.

218

But in closing, let me obviously encourage you to not allow these Global Elites to change who you are as a human being. We were created in God's image, not theirs! Theirs will always be faulty and will always lead to destruction. However, there is a new type of creation I really would encourage you to turn into. Not Human 2.0, the version of these Global Elites, but rather becoming a "new creation" in Jesus Christ.

2 Corinthians 5:17 "Therefore, if anyone is in Christ, he is a new creation; the old has gone, the new has come!"

And the reason why I encourage you to allow that transformation to take place inside of you is because the Bible is clear. We are all infected with this horrible disease called sin. And it is this sin that separates us from a Holy and Righteous God and disqualifies us from having a personal relationship with Him now, as well as forever, in a place called Heaven.

Romans 3:23, 6:23 "For all have sinned and fall short of the glory of God. For the wages of sin is death, but the gift of God is eternal life in Christ Jesus our Lord."

Now, if you're anything like I used to be, you certainly don't like being called a "sinner." In fact, you're probably thinking, at this moment, "Well, I'm not that bad of a person."

Actually, it's pretty easy to demonstrate that you're not sinless, and neither am I for that matter. This is what God's Ten Commandments were all about. They are God's X-ray showing us that we're really disqualified for Heaven. We've sinned.

For instance, how many of you, have ever lied? Which is the 9th commandment. Okay, for those who say you didn't, you just did, you lied, because we've all done that at one time or another.

Or how about this one, the eighth commandment? You shall not steal. How many of you have ever taken something that wasn't yours without permission, ever once? Okay, you already told me you're a bunch of liars, so let's not commit another lie. Because the truth is, we've all stolen or taken something without permission that didn't belong to us.

That's just two out of the Ten Commandments. How are you doing? It's obvious, when you begin to see the X-Ray, that none of us can keep them, which means we all fall short of the glory of God, we have sin, and we're all disqualified for Heaven. We deserve to be separated from God forever.

But the good news is God is willing to "give us the gift of eternal life in Christ Jesus our Lord." In other words, if you would just receive His gift of eternal life by faith and call upon the Name of the Lord Jesus Christ and ask Him to forgive you of all your sins, you too can go to Heaven. In fact, Jesus is the only way to Heaven.

John 14:6 "Jesus answered, I am the way and the truth and the life. No one comes to the Father except through me."

Romans 10:9-10 "For if you confess with your mouth that Jesus is Lord and believe in your heart that God raised him from the dead, you will be saved. For it is by believing in your heart that you are made right with God, and it is by confessing with your mouth that you are saved."

Be encouraged, it really is true. If you would entrust your life to Jesus Christ and call upon the His Name and ask Him to forgive you of all your sins, then you too will become qualified for Heaven.

You see, I'm not going there because I'm perfect. It's simply because I've been forgiven! I became a "new creation" in Christ, because I "received" this "good news" by "faith" almost 30 years ago, when my eyes were "opened" to "see" what the enemy didn't want me to "see."

The fact is we've been horribly lied to by these Global Elites, including the truth about the existence of God and who Jesus Christ really is. And that's why He's given you this evidence today in hopes that you will reverse your thinking before it's too late.

Don't trust the Elites, trust in God. He wants you to experience the gift of eternal life before it's too late. Reverse everything these Global Elites have told you and you will finally see the truth.

Ephesians 2:1-2: "As for you, you were dead in your transgressions and sins, in which you used to live when you followed the ways of this world."

I will live my life according to these beliefs.
God does not exist
It's just foolish to think
That there is an all-knowing God with a cosmic plan.

That an all-powerful God brings purpose to the pain and suffering in the
world
It is a comforting thought however
It is only wishful thinking
People can do as they please without eternal consequences.
The idea that
I am deserving of hell
Because of sin,
Is a lie meant to make me a slave to those in power.
"The more you have, the happier you will be."
Our existence has no grand meaning or purpose.
In a world with no God
There is freedom to be who I want to be
But with God
Life is an endless cycle of guilt and shame
Without God
Everything is fine
It is ridiculous to think
I am lost and in need of saving

And that's how I felt before Christ opened my eyes, changed my heart
And Reversed My Thinking

I am lost and in need of saving
It is ridiculous to think
Everything is fine
Without God
Life is an endless cycle of guilt and shame
But with God
There is freedom to be who I want to be
In a world with no God
Our existence has no grand meaning or purpose
"The more you have, the happier you will be."
Is a lie meant to make me a slave to those in power
Because of sin,
I am deserving of hell

The idea that
People can do as they please without eternal consequences.
Is only wishful thinking
It is a comforting thought however
That an all-powerful God brings purpose to the pain and suffering in the world
That there is an all-knowing God with a cosmic plan.
It's just foolish to think
God does not exist
I will live my life according to these beliefs.

Ephesians 2:4-5: "But because of His great love for us, God who is rich in mercy, made us alive with Christ even when we were dead in transgressions."

Folks, we've been lied to. Please, reverse your thinking before it's too late. God judged this planet once, and He's getting ready to do it again, partly because of what these Global Elites are doing. Please, turn your thinking around and turn to Jesus the only way out of this mess and get saved today before it's too late! God Bless!

How to Receive Jesus Christ:

1. Admit your need (I am a sinner).

2. Be willing to turn from your sins (repent).

3. Believe that Jesus Christ died for you on the Cross and rose from the grave.

4. Through prayer, invite Jesus Christ to come in and control your life through the Holy Spirit. (Receive Him as Lord and Savior.)

What to pray:

Dear Lord Jesus,

I know that I am a sinner and need Your forgiveness. I believe that You died for my sins. I want to turn from my sins. I now invite You to come into my heart and life. I want to trust and follow You as Lord and Savior.

In Jesus' name. Amen.

22

Notes

1. *China people drop Dead. Wuhan. Coronavirus*
https://www.youtube.com/watch?v=3fKTZuY6KxM
2. *Moderna develops vaccine for HIV-AIDS*
https://www.youtube.com/watch?v=WlJgWUzPFLU
3. *Life Simplified with Connected Devices*
https://www.youtube.com/watch?v=NjYTzvAVozo
4. *What is 5G- - CNBC Explains*
https://www.youtube.com/watch?v=2DG3pMcNNlw
5. *ESOF2020 Trieste - Going Viral- – GM viruses in the environment*
https://www.youtube.com/watch?v=8nTKs9EhEWI
6. *"They're Doing WHAT To Our Food-!!" This Is NOT GOOD -*
https://www.youtube.com/watch?v=oZ9RL6aziWE
7. *Plant-based vaccines for COVID-19 and other viruses - COVID-19 Special*
https://www.youtube.com/watch?v=-HkM2ipSD4k
8. *DARPA SBIR- Profusa Implantable Biosensors - COL Matt Hepburn -*
https://www.youtube.com/watch?v=jzOeY2DVHyE
9. *HUMANS 2.0*
https://www.youtube.com/watch?v=fXB5-iwNah0
10. *Humans 2.0- Panel Discussion Highlights - WEF 2019 in Davos*
https://www.youtube.com/watch?v=8GI1SI2ED1M&t=131s
11. *Pfizer, Biontech Covid-19 Vaccine Uses Technology That Could Revolutionize Future Immunizations*
https://www.youtube.com/watch?v=9Vrd9Ip9BDM
12. *Graphene oxide*
https://www.youtube.com/watch?v=Soe__9hCBcM
13. *Graphene Oxide and EMF's*
https://www.youtube.com/watch?v=EU6e3I9glPk
14. *Graphene oxide cell phone*
https://www.youtube.com/watch?v=tOApJPbmUsk
15. *Nanotubes assemble! Rice introduces Teslaphoresis*

https://www.youtube.com/watch?v=w1d0Lg6wuvc
16. *Self-Assembling Wires*
https://www.youtube.com/watch?v=PeHWqr9dz3c
17. *Sequencing DNA with Graphene*
https://www.youtube.com/watch?v=bsXJ_EJsh-E
18. *What's Graphene And Why It'll Soon Take Over The World*
https://www.youtube.com/watch?v=dQCJpYR0og8
19. *Wonder material graphene connects to a 5G network, coffee machines and self-driving cars*
https://www.youtube.com/watch?v=-6CP8-fDdc0
20. *Graphene micromotors spin forward*
https://www.youtube.com/watch?v=00sRZL11wzo
21. *Graphene oxide - Black Goo More Predictive Programming*
https://www.youtube.com/watch?v=SAx91YiWdSY
22. *Nanotechnology- Hacking Humans, Its Potential, and Real Risks*
https://www.youtube.com/watch?v=nsGvcejqzb4
23. *Self-Assembling Wires*
https://www.youtube.com/watch?v=PeHWqr9dz3c
24. *Australian Covid Quarantine Camps- Is THIS The Future*
https://www.youtube.com/watch?v=tBHkd3sXxT8
25. *Canadian details 'traumatic' stay in a quarantine facility - COVID-19 restrictions*
https://www.youtube.com/watch?v=OxewIciTUoE
26. *Concern grows as more countries detect monkeypox - DW News*
https://www.youtube.com/watch?v=nKGNUcAHqoI
27. *Coronavirus Outbreak- Life inside quarantine camps*
https://www.youtube.com/watch?v=-0qnUhvQelk
28. *Covid-19- China puts people in 'metal boxes' at quarantine camps - Oneindia News*
https://www.youtube.com/watch?v=kRey9L_-_4g
29. *Drone footage shows sheer scale of Auschwitz death camp*
https://www.youtube.com/watch?v=lafLo1Gdp5o
30. *HAARP CBC Broadcast Weather control part 1*
https://www.youtube.com/watch?v=QkLTzesBxGE
31. *HAARP CBC Broadcast Weather control part 2*
https://www.youtube.com/watch?v=Zi1nLmlicxU

32. *Inside Australia's Covid internment camp*
https://www.youtube.com/watch?v=mGFdWcJU7-0
33. *Marburg- The Completely Untreatable Virus*
https://www.youtube.com/watch?v=PW5szSKoIdU
34. *People Forced Quarantine In Tiny Metal Boxes Under China's Zero Covid Rule*
https://www.youtube.com/watch?v=-6-ZmUcB6ZI
35. *Tucker- Canada sending COVID positive travelers to 'internment' facilities*
https://www.youtube.com/watch?v=QDIfFb5z7eQ
36. *What Elon Musk's 42,000 Satellites Could Do To Earth*
https://www.youtube.com/watch?v=Aw3R-4UC4wI
37. *4 Ways Nanotechnology Will Change Our Lives*
https://www.youtube.com/watch?v=dn2UjBIsrcI
38. *Cell regeneration- Nanochip can regrow organs, heal injuries with just one touch - TomoNews*
https://www.youtube.com/watch?v=_nar6vX6OJ4
39. *China reportedly trying to make super soldiers; Gen Keane reacts*
https://www.youtube.com/watch?v=KBEYOZzoThA
40. *Gravitas- China's unconventional war- -Brain Control weapons- for Super Soldiers*
https://www.youtube.com/watch?v=3WfzxgiM2WI
41. *Gravitas- Is China breeding genetically modified soldiers*
https://www.youtube.com/watch?v=19811iKYBZM
42. *Gravitas- North Korean Soldiers with 'iron fists' showcase their might*
https://www.youtube.com/watch?v=RQKgfwRkFAQ
43. *In Future, US Creates The Most Genius Android Super Soldier To Help Ukraine Against Russia*
https://www.youtube.com/watch?v=DGFcXxiAwTc
44. *Lucy TRAILER 1 (2014) - Luc Besson, Scarlett Johansson Movie HD*
https://www.youtube.com/watch?v=MVt32qoyhi0
45. *Mysterious Virus Turns The Infected Into Zombies With a Superhuman Strength*
https://www.youtube.com/watch?v=uF3vU4tYaqg
46. *Real Life Super Soldier Program*
https://www.youtube.com/watch?v=07-OZFEAJAo

47. THE -NANITES- for FUTURE SOLDIER - VIN DIESEL - GUY PIERCE - BLOODSHOT (2020)
https://www.youtube.com/watch?v=XBNwPNS9XCQ
48. The Strongest Super Soldiers Russia Ever Created, Each Can Take Down 100 Soldiers
https://www.youtube.com/watch?v=EMAkon6j1Rk
49. The Super Soldier Serum Explained 2021 - MCU Lore
https://www.youtube.com/watch?v=N8tPd6rR3CI
50. Top 5 Advanced Nano-Tech inventions that will change the world#Nanomedicine nanotechnology#
https://www.youtube.com/watch?v=xgPbKWVJFEM
51. U.S. Official Says China Attempted To Create 'Super Soldiers' - Hallie Jackson - MSNBC
https://www.youtube.com/watch?v=K31L-fkJZ-I
52. Zombie movies
https://www.youtube.com/results?search_query=zombie+movies
53. Elon Musk - You can turn someone into a frickin butterfly with the right rna - dna sequence.
https://www.youtube.com/watch?v=Ui0k1Px1NGM
54. Elon Musk Reveals New Details About Neuralink, His Brain Implant Technology
https://www.youtube.com/watch?v=Gqdo57uky4o
55. Elon Musk says you can turn someone into a butterfly with mRNA
https://www.youtube.com/watch?v=Ges2yk2PNcA
56. The Fourth Industrial Revolution - At a glance
https://www.youtube.com/watch?v=KP9sMNwf6zw
57. The Matrix - The War Between Man and Machine
https://www.youtube.com/watch?v=wSh8tk6NAAg
58. What is the Fourth Industrial Revolution- by Prof Klaus Schwab
https://www.youtube.com/watch?v=7xUk1F7dyvI
59. Yuval Noah Harari - Transhumanism and Eliminating Free Will
https://www.youtube.com/watch?v=QuL3wlodJC8
60. Yuval Noah Harari - -We Don't Need to Wait for Jesus Christ In-Order to Overcome Death
https://www.youtube.com/watch?v=hs2aPGxlV34

51. *A global catastrophe'- Radiation activist warns that 5G networks are 'massive health experiment'*
https://www.rt.com/news/450775-massive-health-experiment-5g-cancer/

52. *5G and EMF Health Hazards - SPOTLIGHT with Tina Griffin*
https://rumble.com/vr305d-5g-and-emf-health-hazards-spotlight-with-tina-griffin.html

53. *5G Apocalypse- The Extinction Event film reveals how 5G is an assault weapon meant to destroy humanity*
https://www.naturalnews.com/2019-05-19-5g-apocalypse-extinction-event-film-destroy-humanity.html

54. *5G Is Coming, And With It Potentially Calamitous Health Risks*
https://prepforthat.com/5g-health-risks/

55. *5G, Biometrics Systems Being Covertly Installed In Schools During Coronavirus Lockdowns*
https://www.silverdoctors.com/headlines/world-news/5g-biometrics-systems-being-covertly-installed-in-schools-during-coronavirus-lockdowns/

56. *Corona Investigative Committee*
https://corona-investigative-committee.com/about/

57. *Africa to Become Test bed for Gates Funded Biometric ID system*
https://oye.news/news/world-news/africa-to-become-test-bed-for-gates-funded-biometric-id-system/

58. *Africa to Become Testing Ground for -Trust Stamp- Vaccine Record and Payment System*
https://www.mintpressnews.com/africa-trust-stamp-covid-19-vaccine-record-payment-system/269346/

59. *Article- During Shutdown 5G Being Installed Covertly in US Schools, Dept of Education Directive*
https://www.opednews.com/articles/During-Shutdown-5G-Being-I-by-Beverly-Jensen-Absence_Dept-Of-Education-ED-gov_Education_Educational-Facilities-200322-906.html

70. *Attorney Todd Callender- The Vax Genocide Has Likely Killed a Billion People*
https://freedomfirstnetwork.com/2022/02/attorney-todd-callender-the-vax-genocide-has-likely-killed-a-billion-people

71. *Attorney Tom Renz Discovers Leaked DOD COVID Files*

ttps://renz-law.com/attorney-tom-renz-discovers-leaked-dod-covid-files/
72. *Beware of typhus. Avoid Jews.- poster from the German-occupied region of Poland, early 1940s*
https://imgur.com/g89Sfgu
73. *Bioweapon Injections Loaded With Nanotech & Covid Camps Expanded For Dissention*
https://rumble.com/v13wp5t-bioweapon-injections-loaded-with-nanotech-and-covid-camps-expanded-for-diss.html
74. *Brighteon*
https://www.brighteon.com/2f73de6e-80ba-4c58-8dfd-08bac350e707
75. *Cancer vaccine using same tech as Covid jabs could be a 'game-changer'*
https://www.msn.com/en-gb/health/medical/cancer%20vaccine%20using%20same%20tech%20as%20covid%20jabs%20could%20be%20a%20'game-changer'/ar-AAWlida
76. *CDC announces covid internment camps for every US city*
https://speakingaboutnews.com/cdc-announces-covid-internment-camps-for-every-us-city/
77. *Complete List of Zombie Movies*
https://www.imdb.com/list/ls059468572/?sort=release_date,desc&st_dt=&mode=grid&page=1&ref_=ttls_vw_grd
78. *Contagious Vaccines- — Mandates by Mad Science.*
https://rumble.com/vyv204-contagious-vaccines-mandates-by-mad-science.html
79. *Corona Investigative Committee*
https://corona-investigative-committee.com/
80. *COVID UPDATE- What is the truth*
https://www.ncbi.nlm.nih.gov/pmc/articles/PMC9062939/
81. *COVID-19 Vaccine AstraZeneca*
https://www.fda.gov.ph/wp-content/uploads/2021/02/PI-for-COVID-19-Vaccine-AstraZeneca.pdf
82. *COVID-19 vaccine spike proteins are SHEDDING, giving people heart attacks, strokes and more*
https://www.newstarget.com/2022-01-18-covid-vaccine-spike-proteins-shedding-unvaccinated.html
83. *DANGERS OF 5G PART 2*

https://rumble.com/vunbb2-dangers-of-5g-part-2.html
84. *DARPA Funds Brain-Stimulation Research to Speed Learning - U.S. Department of Defense - Defense Department News*
https://www.defense.gov/News/News-Stories/Article/Article/1164793/darpa-funds-brain-stimulation-research-to-speed-learning/
85. *DARPA Hydrogel in COVID Vaccine can create crystals, nano-antennas to receive signals from 5G Tower*
https://spacetravelinalabama.wordpress.com/2021/05/19/darpa-hydrogel-in-covid-vaccine-can-create-crystals-nano-antennas-to-receive-signals-from-5g-tower/
86. *DARPA's New Project Is Investing Millions in Brain-Machine*
https://singularityhub.com/2019/06/05/darpas-new-project-is-investing-millions-in-brain-machine-interface-tech/Interface Tech
87. *Death Shot- 1000% Increase in Vaccine Deaths And Injuries Among Children Post-Covid Vaccination*
https://winepressnews.com/2022/04/18/death-shot-1000-increase-in-vaccine-deaths-and-injuries-among-children-post-covid-vaccination/
88. *Did the 5G rollout in Wuhan damage the innate cellular defense cells of the population, putting the people at risk of complications and death from coronavirus?*
https://www.radiation.news/2020-02-26-5g-rollout-in-wuhan-damage-the-innate-cellular-defense-cells-coronavirus.html
89. *Dr Charles Hoffe Reveals Canada's Covid Vaccine Deaths & Injuries VAERS Report*
https://rumble.com/vu4e0z-dr-charles-hoffe-reveals-canadas-covid-vaccine-deaths-and-injuries-vaers-re.html
90. *Dr. Elizabeth Eads - -Millions Will Get AIDS From the Covid Vaccine By Fall 2022*
https://rumble.com/vyyg64-dr.-elizabeth-eads-millions-will-get-aids-from-the-covid-vaccine-by-fall.html
91. *FDA report finds all-cause mortality higher among vaccinated - Israel National News*
https://www.israelnationalnews.com/news/317091
92. *FINALLY-Everything you wanted to know about 5G and Radiation (Documentary)*

https://rumble.com/vteqe3-finally-everything-you-wanted-to-know-about-5g-and-radiation-documentary.html
93. *Foreign Materials Found in Moderna Vaccine May Be Metal*
https://www.nippon.com/en/news/yjj2021082601094/
94. *Gates-funded Program to Begin Tests on Biometric ID Vaccination Records in Africa*
https://thenewamerican.com/gates-funded-program-to-begin-tests-on-biometric-id-vaccination-records-in-africa/
95. *GAVI*
https://en.wikipedia.org/wiki/GAVI
96. *Global Health Agencies Planned for Monkeypox Pandemic to Strike in May 2022, Wargame Document from Early 2021 Reveals*
https://beckernews.com/monkeypox-nti-wargame-45055/
97. *HHS Issues New PREP Act Immunity to Marburgvirus Countermeasures - Publications - Insights - Faegre Drinker Biddle & Reath*
https://www.faegredrinker.com/en/insights/publications/2020/12/hhs-issues-new-prep-act-immunity-to-marburgvirus-countermeasures
98. *How Human Brains Could Be Hacked*
https://www.livescience.com/37938-how-human-brain-could-be-hacked.html
99. *Interim Operational Considerations for Implementing the Shielding Approach to Prevent COVID-19 Infections in Humanitarian*
https://www.cdc.gov/coronavirus/2019-ncov/global-covid-19/shielding-approach-humanitarian.html
100. *Japan discovers "magnetic" substance in Pfizer covid vaccines; journalists start DYING from the vax they pushed*
https://canadianmale.wordpress.com/2021/08/28/japan-discovers-magnetic-substance-in-pfizer-covid-vaccines-journalists-start-dying-from-the-vax-they-pushed/
101. *Japan Suspends 1.6 Million Doses of Moderna Vaccine After Reports of Contamination*
https://www.theepochtimes.com/japan-suspends-1-63-million-doses-of-moderna-vaccine-after-reports-of-contamination_3966233.html
102. *Leading German Chemist Andreas Noack Dies 30 Minutes After Exposing Graphene Oxide, Possibly Assassinated*

https://www.eutimes.net/2021/12/leading-german-chemist-andreas-noack-dies-30-minutes-after-exposing-graphene-oxide-possibly-assassinated/
103. *May 7, 2022*
https://rumble.com/v13u8pv-may-7-2022.html
104. *Military programs aiming to end pandemics forever*
https://www.cbsnews.com/news/last-pandemic-science-military-60-minutes-2021-04-11/
105. *Moderna's Coronavirus Treatment Transforms Body Into Vaccine-Making Machine*
https://www.bloomberg.com/features/2020-moderna-biontech-covid-shot/
106. *Monkeypox Was a Table-Top Simulation Only Last Year*
https://brownstone.org/articles/monkeypox-was-a-table-top-simulation-only-last-year/
107. *New Dr. Carrie Madej- -Immortal- Hydra Vulgaris In Moderna's Vaccine- Startling Microscope Findings*
https://beforeitsnews.com/prophecy/2021/10/new-dr-carrie-madej-immortal-hydra-vulgaris-in-modernas-vaccine-startling-microscope-findings-2524400.html
108. *New Stew Peters- Shocking! Dr. Carrie Madej Releases First Look at Pfizer Vial Contents*
https://beforeitsnews.com/prophecy/2021/10/new-stew-peters-shocking-dr-carrie-madej-releases-first-look-at-pfizer-vial-contents-2524862.html
109. *Next pandemic could be 'more contagious, or more lethal, or both,' vaccine co-creator warns*
https://news.yahoo.com/next-pandemic-could-more-contagious-112522394.html
110. *On the Agenda - Human Enhancement - World Economic Forum*
https://www.weforum.org/agenda/human-enhancement
111. *Part 1. Barrie Trower – Lecture- 'The Truth about 5G and Wi-Fi*
https://multerland.wpcomstaging.com/2020/09/11/barrie-trower-lecture-the-truth-about-5g-and-wi-fi/
112. *Promising cancer vaccine in the works utilizing similar mRNA technology that combats COVID- Duke researchers*
https://www.foxnews.com/health/promising-cancer-vaccine-utilizing-similar-mrna-technology-combats-covid-duke-researchers
113. *Replication-defective vector based on a chimpanzee adenovirus*

https://pubmed.ncbi.nlm.nih.gov/11689642/
114. *Researchers aim to develop edible plant-based mRNA vaccines*
https://www.news-medical.net/news/20210916/Researchers-aim-to-develop-edible-plant-based-mRNA-vaccines.aspx
115. *Rumble Downloader - Online Rumble Video Downloader - YTGRAM.com.url"*
https://ytgram.com/en/rumble-video-downloader#url=https://rumble.com/vusutm-dr-li-meng-yan-reveals-ccp-spreading-hemorrhagic-fever-bioweapon-via-olympi.html
116. *Scientists are working to develop plants that can deliver mRNA vaccine technology*
https://www.dailymail.co.uk/health/article-10013497/Scientists-working-develop-plants-deliver-mRNA-vaccine-technology.html
117. *Scientists Developing Contagious Vaccines That Can Spread From Vaxxed To Unvaxxed*
https://rumble.com/vymwjw-scientists-developing-contagious-vaccines-that-can-spread-from-vaxxed-to-un.html
118. *Scientists Developing Controversial 'Contagious Vaccines' Designed as "Recombinant Viruses" That Spread From Vaccinated to Unvaccinated*
https://newsrescue.com/scientists-developing-controversial-contagious-vaccines-designed-as-recombinant-viruses-that-spread-from-vaccinated-to-unvaccinated/
119. *Secret DARPA Mind Control Project Revealed- Leaked Document*
https://prepareforchange.net/2018/12/16/secret-darpa-mind-control-project-revealed-leaked-document/
120. *Self-Spreading Vaccines Do Not Require Your Consent*
https://rumble.com/vxcvph-self-spreading-vaccines-do-not-require-your-consent.html
121. *SHEDDING DANGER- 12-Year-Old Girl Injured by Vaxxed Dad*
https://rumble.com/vpdlq3-shedding-dad-injures-daughter-doctor-says-vaxxed-father-making-daughter-sic.html
122. *Shedding is Real But Is It Dangerous*
https://rumble.com/vw4cc6-shedding-is-real-but-is-it-dangerous.html
123. *Strategic Intelligence*
https://intelligence.weforum.org/topics/a1G0X000006NvAbUAK

124. *Study- COVID-19 Vaccines INCREASE Deaths and Hospitalizations from COVID-19 Based on Analysis of Most-Vaccinated Countries*
https://peckford42.wordpress.com/2021/10/01/study-covid-19-vaccines-increase-deaths-and-hospitalizations-from-covid-19-based-on-analysis-of-most-vaccinated-countries/

125. *The COVID vaccines have triggered a global AIDS pandemic*
https://rumble.com/vyl2gx-the-covid-vaccines-have-triggered-a-global-aids-pandemic..html

126. *The next pandemic- Marburg- - Gavi, the Vaccine Alliance*
https://www.gavi.org/vaccineswork/next-pandemic/marburg

127. *THOMAS RENZ - THE COVERUP PHASE HAS BEGUN, THE EVIDENCE WILL BRING DOWN BIG PHARMA & FAUCI*
https://trusttheq.com/thomas-renz-the-coverup-phase-has-begun-the-evidence-will-bring-down-big-pharma-fauci/

128. *Todd Callender - Session 97- Open Secrets*
https://odysee.com/@Corona-Investigative-Committee:5/Session-97-Todd-Callender:0

129. *Todd Callender- The Role of Hospitals, Covid Injections And 5G In Genocide - Truth for Health Foundation*
https://www.truthforhealth.org/2022/04/todd-callender-the-role-of-hospitals-covid-injections-and-5g-in-genocide/

130. *Total Population Control*
https://educate-yourself.org/mc/mctotalcontrol12jul02.shtml

131. *US, Europe, Australia, monkeypox is spreading- Can the virus lead to a pandemic*
https://www.firstpost.com/health/us-europe-australia-monkeypox-is-spreading-can-the-virus-lead-to-a-pandemic-10699351.html

132. *Vaccines of the future could be as contagious as viruses*
https://www.popsci.com/contagious-vaccine-virus/

133. *Vax Induced Mass Death- Funeral Director Predicts Covid Camps and Jab Genocide*
https://rumble.com/vrpq4l-vax-induced-mass-death-funeral-director-predicts-covid-camps-and-jab-genoci.html

134. *Weaponized Viruses Exposed- Mind-Blowing Discovery About HIV, SARS, & Marburg*

https://rumble.com/vv78jm-weaponized-viruses-exposed-mind-blowing-discovery-about-hiv-sars-and-marbur.html

135. *WHAT YOU NEED TO KNOW ABOUT COVID-19 VACCINE SPIKE PROTEIN SHEDDING*
https://rumble.com/v11weww-what-you-need-to-know-about-covid-19-vaccine-spike-protein-shedding.html

136. *Whistleblower Doctor MURDERED After Exposing Graphene Oxide in Bioweapon Shots!*
https://rumble.com/vq4ms2-whistleblower-doctor-attacked-killed-after-exposing-graphene-in-shots.html

137. *Who is Viviane Fischer*
https://int.artloft.co/who-is-viviane-fischer/

138. *You searched for monkeypox – The Vault Project*
https://thevaultproject.org/?s=monkeypox

139. *Yuval Noah Harari - Top Klaus Schwab Advisor Explains -The Dangers of Free-Will*
https://rumble.com/vwuorf-yuval-noah-harari-top-klaus-schwab-advisor-explains-the-dangers-of-free-wil.html

Lightning Source UK Ltd.
Milton Keynes UK
UKHW020757210722
406179UK00010B/976